A Twist of Faith

A Twist of Faith

by

Berit Kjos

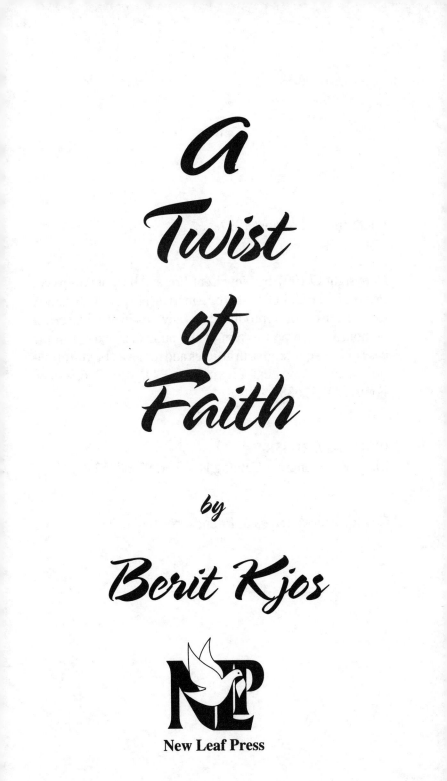

New Leaf Press

First printing: August 1997

ISBN: 0-89221-358-2
Library of Congress Catalog Number: 97-68952

Cover by Steve Diggs & Friends, Nashville, TN.

Table of Contents

Chapter 1

Our Father in Heaven,
or
Our Mother, the Earth?

❦

Our Maker Sophia, we are women in your image.[1] (Over 2,000 "Christian" women praising a feminine alternative to God)

I am the goddess! We are the goddess![2] (About 700 women dancing around a totem pole in Mankato, Minnesota)

O Great Spirit, earth and wind and sea, you are inside and all around me. (Sung at the Re-Imagining Conference, Girl Scout camp, etc.)

My people have committed two sins: They have forsaken me, the spring of living water, and have dug their own cisterns, broken cisterns that cannot hold water. (Jer. 2:13)

❦

Peggy's struggles seemed endless. She wanted to be close to God, but she rarely felt His presence. She wanted her teenage son to love Him, but the occult posters in his room became daily reminders of unanswered prayer. She joined a Christian ministry, but satisfying fellowship with God kept eluding her. Eventually she left the ministry to return to college.

She called me a few years later. She had begun to find herself, she said. Her search had led her beyond the familiar voices that had provided "pat answers" to her spiritual questions. The biblical God no longer seemed relevant or benevolent. A college teacher had been especially helpful in her journey toward self-discovery. This teacher-counselor called herself a witch — one who believes in the power of magic formulas and rituals to invoke power from spiritual forces.

Some years passed. When she called again, she had left her husband and moved away. "I had to find *me*," she explained. "My spiritual journey has opened my eyes to a whole new paradigm. . . ."

"A new paradigm?"

"Yes. A brand new way of seeing God and myself — and everything else. It's like being born again."

"Who is Jesus Christ to you now?" I asked.

"He is a symbol of redemption," she answered. "But I haven't rejected the Bible. I'm only trying to make my spiritual experience my own. I have to hear my own voice and not let someone else choose for me. Meanwhile, I'm willing to live with confusion and mystery, and I feel like I'm in God's hands whether God is He, She, or It."

Can you identify with Peggy? Or do you have friends on similar journeys? Like millions of other seekers, Peggy longs for practical spirituality, a sense of identity, a community of like-minded seekers, and a God she can feel. She remembers meaningful Bible verses, but they have lost their authority as guidelines. Somehow the Bible no longer fits her thinking, nor her personal wants.

She wonders why God isn't more tolerant and broadminded. After all, He is the God of love, isn't He? Maybe a feminine deity would be more compassionate, understanding, and relevant to women. Perhaps it's time to move beyond the old boundaries of biblical truth into the boundless realms of dreams, visions, and self-discovery?

Multitudes have. What used to be sparsely traveled sideroads to New Age experiences have become cultural freeways to self-made spirituality. Masses of church women drift onto these mystical superhighways where they adapt their former beliefs to today's more "inclusive" views. After all, they are told, peace in a pluralistic world demands a more open-minded look at *all* religions and cultures.

Those who agree can find countless paths to self-discovery and personal empowerment through books, magazines, and new kinds of women's group. They meet at the YWCA, in bookstores, in traditional churches, at retreat centers, living rooms . . . anywhere. Here, strange new words and ideas — such as "enneagrams," Sophia Circles, global consciousness, and "critical mass" — offer modern formulas for spiritual transformation. Therapists, spiritual directors, and others promise "safe places" where seekers can discover *their own* truth, learn new rituals, affirm each other's experiences, and free themselves from old rules and limitations.

Perhaps you are part of such a group. You may have friends or relatives who are exploring these new paths. Or you may be among those who wonder how those weird, mystical activities could possibly touch *your* life. Unlike the women seeking truth in pagan circles, you may know your destination and sense no need for spiritual alternatives. You are safe in your family, in your church, among your personal friends. . . .

Are you sure? This new spiritual movement is transforming our churches as well as our culture. It touches every family that reads newspapers, watches television, and sends children to community schools. It is fast driving our society beyond Christianity, beyond humanism — even beyond relativism — toward new global beliefs and values. No one is immune from its subtle pressures and silent promptings. That it parallels other social changes and global movements only speeds the transformation. Yet, most Christians — like the proverbial frog — have barely noticed.

This feminist movement demands new deities or, at least, a re-thinking of the old ones. The transformation starts with self, some say, and women can't re-invent themselves until they shed the old shackles. So the search for a "more relevant" religion requires new visions of God: images that trade holiness for tolerance, the heavenly for the earthly, and the God who is higher than us for a god who *is* us.

The most seductive images are feminine. They may look like postcard angels, fairy godmothers, Greek earth goddesses, radiant New Age priestesses, or even a mythical Mary, but they all promise unconditional love, peace, power, and personal transcendence. To many, they seem too good to refuse.

The Seductive Masks of the Feminine Gods

You probably wouldn't expect to find goddesses in a conservative farming community in North Dakota. I didn't. But one day when visiting my husband's rural hometown, a neighbor told us that a new bookstore had just opened in the parsonage of the old Lutheran Church. "You should go see it," she urged.

I agreed, so I drove to a stately white church, walked to the parsonage next door, and rang the bell. The pastor's wife opened the door and led me into a large room she had changed into a bookstore, leaving me to browse. Scanning the shelves along the walls, I noticed familiar authors such as Lynn Andrews who freely blends witchcraft with Native American rituals, New Age self-empowerment, and other occult traditions to form *her own* spirituality.

Among the multicultural books in the children's section, one caught my attention. Called *Many Faces of the*

Great Goddess, it was a " coloring book for all ages." Page after page sported voluptuous drawings of famed goddesses. Nude, bare-breasted, pregnant, or draped in serpents, they would surely open the minds of young artists to the lure of "sacred" sex and ancient myths.

Driving home, I pondered today's fast-spreading shift from Christianity to paganism. Apparently, myths and spiritualized sensuality sound good to those who seek new revelations and "higher" truths. Many of the modern myths picture deities that fit somewhere between a feminine version of God and the timeless goddesses pictured in earth-centered stories and cultures. Yet, each can be tailor-made to fit the diverse tastes and demands of today's searching women:

- *Angels.* Terry wears an angel pin on her jacket. She believes that today's popular angels offer all kinds of personal help, guidance and encouragement. While God seems distant and impersonal to her, she counts on her personal angel to help and love her. She showed me a set of angel cards on a rack in her gift store. "May this Guardian Angel . . . give you hope and strength to meet each new tomorrow," suggested a sympathy card, complete with a tiny golden angel pin.

- *Sophia.* "Sophia, Creator God, let your milk and honey flow. . . . Shower us with your love," chanted more than 2,000 women gathered at the 1993 Re-Imagining Conference in Minnesota. "We celebrate sensual life you give us. . . . We celebrate our bodiliness. . . . the sensations of pleasure, our oneness with earth and water,"[3] continued one of the leaders. Representing mainline denominations, the women had come from the Presbyterian Church USA (about 400), the United Methodist Church (about 400), the Evangelical Lutheran Church of America (313), the United Church of Christ (144), and Baptist, Episcopal, Church of the Brethren churches (about 150). More than 200 were Roman Catholics. To most of these worshippers, Sophia symbolized inner wisdom and "the feminine image of the Divine." Playful, permissive, and sensuous, she has "become the latest rage among progressive church women."[4]

• *Mother Earth.* Tracy is a regional Girl Scout leader in Santa Clara County, California. To prepare young girls for an "Initiation into adulthood" ceremony, she uses guided imagery to alter their consciousness and help them visualize a "beautiful woman" — a personalized expression of Mother Earth — who will be their spirit guide for life. Each girl is free to imagine the spiritual manifestation of her choice or to welcome whichever spirit appears.

• *A goddess.* Sharon grew up in a Christian home. Disappointed with her church's chilly response to her environmental concerns, she turned to witchcraft. Since her coven accepts any pantheistic expression, Sharon simply transferred what she liked about God to her self-made image of the goddess. She describes her feminine substitute for God as a loving, non-judgmental being who fills all of creation with her sacred life. Sometimes this goddess appears to Sharon, bathing her in bright light and a loving presence.

These and countless other women share two radical views: traditional Christianity with its biblical boundaries are *out,* and boundless new vistas of spiritual thrills and skills are *in.* Anything goes — except biblical monotheism, belief in one God. The broad umbrella of feminist spirituality covers all of the world's pagan religions and many of today's popular distortions of Christianity. Most seekers simply pick and mix the "best parts" of several traditions. Someone might start with Buddhist meditation, then add

Chinese medicine, Hindu yoga, and a Native American wilderness initiation called "Spirit Quest." Some of these combinations match today's feminist visions better than others, but most involve the following:

Pantheism: All is god. A spirit, force, energy or god(dess) permeates everything, infusing all parts of creation with its spiritual life.

Monism: All is one. Since the pantheistic god *is* everything and *in* everyone, all things are connected.

Polytheism: Many gods. Since the pantheistic force or god(dess) makes everything sacred, anything can be worshipped: the sun, trees, mountains and eagles — even ourselves.

Paganism: Trusting occult wisdom and powers. Throughout history, tribal shamans, medicine men, witchdoctors, or priests have contacted the spirit world using timeless rituals and formulas which are surprisingly similar in all the world's pagan cultures.

Neo-paganism: New idealized blends of old pagan religions. To make paganism attractive in today's self-focused atmosphere, its promoters idealize tribal cultures and pagan religions. Instead of telling the whole truth and nothing but, they tell us that spiritual forces link each person to every other part of nature. Anyone, not just spiritual leaders, can now function as priestess, contact the spirit world, manipulate spiritual forces, and help create worldwide peace and spiritual oneness.

Gateways to the Goddess

Like most neo-pagans, Diane believes that earth-centered spirituality brings peace and personal empowerment. A pretty young woman with long black hair and the slender look of a vegetarian, she is a local hairdresser. She is also married, looking forward to starting a family, and a member of the Bay Area Pagan Assemblies. While cutting my hair one day, she told me how she discovered the goddess who empowers her.

"I always liked to read," she said, "especially books about magic and witchcraft."

"Which was your favorite?" I asked.

"Margot Adler's book, *Drawing Down the Moon*."

"That's almost an encyclopedia on witchcraft. How old were you?"

"A senior in high school."

"How did you find it?"

"Browsing around in the library. But I had already read some other books, like *Medicine Woman* by Lynn Andrews."

My thoughts drifted to another young woman who read *Medicine Woman* some years ago. Lori's high school teacher had encouraged her to explore various spiritual traditions — even create *her own* religion. Fascinated with Lynn Andrews' blend of Native American shamanism and goddess spirituality, Lori ordered a Native American tipi from a catalog, set it up in her backyard, and used it for candle-lit rituals inspired by Wiccan magic (witchcraft). Like most contemporary pagans, she had learned to mix various traditions into a personal expression that fit her own quest for power and "wisdom from within."

Some months before Diane first cut my hair, I had met a charming Stanford University student who also called herself pagan. Beth, an education and philosophy major, had read my book about environmental spirituality and wanted to discuss it with me. While we ate lunch together at the college cafeteria, she shared her beliefs.

"Who introduced you to witchcraft and lesbianism?" I asked after a while.

"Two of my high school teachers," she answered.

I wasn't surprised. By then I knew that an inordinate number of pagan women have chosen the classroom as their platform for spreading their faith and transforming our culture.[5] Like the rest of us, they want to build a better world — one that reflects *their* beliefs and values.

While Beth talked, I glanced at her jewelry. The golden pentagram and voluptuous little goddess dangling from a chain around her neck spoke volumes about her values. So did her earrings: two large pink triangles pointing down, an ancient symbol of the goddess as well as a modern symbol of lesbianism.

"What about your jewelry?" I asked. "Do people know what the pentagram and triangles symbolize? Do they criticize you for wearing the little goddess?"

She smiled. "No. Everybody here is supposed to be tolerant of each other's lifestyles. Nobody would dare say anything."

I pondered her statement. What does it mean to be tolerant — or intolerant — these days? If intolerance is the self-righteous attitude that despises people with "different" values, it would be wrong. Jesus always demonstrated love and compassion toward the excluded and hurting women of His times. Yet, He never condoned destructive lifestyles or actions that harmed others. What would happen in a culture that tolerates *everything*?

One result is obvious. The last three decades have produced an unprecedented openness to what used to be forbidden realms. Fortunetelling, occult board games, and Native American rituals, along with countless other door-ways to paganism, have spread from the hidden chambers of professional occultists and tribal shamans to our nation's classrooms, environmental programs, Girl Scout camps, and churches.

Leading "Christian" theologians no longer hide their spiritual preference. "The deconstruction of patriarchal religion — in bland terms, the assisted suicide of God the Father — left many of us bereft of divinity," explains feminist theologian Mary Hunt. "But the human hunger for meaning and value . . . finds new expression in goddess worship."[6]

This human hunger for meaning was designed to draw

people to God. He created us to need *Him,* not man-made counterfeits. As the 17th-century philosopher Blaise Pascal wrote, "There's a God-shaped vacuum in every heart." But an astounding number of seekers try to fill that void with seductive substitutes.

Celebrating the Goddess

On June 2, 1994, this spiritual longing brought hundreds of women to San Francisco's Renaissance of the Sacred Feminine Conference. Belying the nearness of summer solstice, a chilly wind swept along the stony walls of Grace Cathedral as I waited with the swelling crowd lining the sidewalk—and prayed.

It grew colder. We buttoned our jackets and huddled together. Some of us studied the program. The cover featured a sensual goddess dancing in front of a large circle — perhaps a sacred sun, or a Buddhist wheel of life, or a Sioux medicine wheel. . . . It didn't matter which. Today's goddess is universal enough to encompass all the world's earth-centered religions and female deities.

An introductory paragraph suggested that this pantheistic goddess would unify people and save the planet: "This participatory event celebrates and honors the presence of the Divine Mother at the heart of the emerging global civilization. The Sacred Feminine has a central role in the healing of our divided minds and endangered planet. . . . Without spiritual transformation on a massive and unprecedented scale, humankind will not survive. . . ."

No survival without an occult transformation?

I looked at the faces around me. People were growing impatient. The 6:30 p.m. entrance time had come and gone, and their pleas for shelter inside had fallen on unsympathetic ears. "Remember we're on a cyclical path, not linear like the old patriarchal ways," was the only excuse given.

I smiled, hoping that goddess-spirituality would continue to prove its true colors.

Twenty-five minutes late the doors flew open and the crowd rushed in, filling the large Episcopal cathedral. While eerie chants to Mother Earth echoed between the gothic pillars, I glanced at a green slip of paper someone handed me at the door. "Failure," it said.

Curious, I turned to a woman next to me and whispered, "What did you get?"

The woman read her green slip and frowned. "Slavery!"

"Ah Ma-*ma*! Ah Ma-*ma*! Ah Ma-*ma*," chanted the Bay Area Lesbian Chorale Ensemble.

As others joined the chant, a large screen flashed pictures of goddesses from around the world. The images ranged from voluptuous fertility goddesses to gruesome blood-guzzling avengers demanding human sacrifice.

The goddess is supposed to be kind and compassionate, I thought. *Yet, in many of her own myths she is cruel beyond words.*

A voice summoned the presence of the many-faced goddess: "Salutations to the great empress who came out of the fire of pure consciousness. . . ." Silently, I kept praising God. Then Alan Jones, dean of the cathedral, shared his delight in our "post-traditional" culture and "the new ways and forms to express the spirit."

A four-step journey toward conscious oneness with this "sacred feminine" began with surrender: "We bow to your sacred power, the holy wisdom of Sophia, our beloved mother who is in heaven and earth. . . ."

"Our Father in Heaven," I prayed silently. *"Holy is Your Name. . . ."*

The second step, Chaos and Ordeal, meant *experiencing* the "ordeals of birth, womb, and transformation." We were told to *imagine* the condition written on our green slips of paper, *enter* its darkness, *feel* the pain, *invoke* the dark mother goddess, then groan, weep and wail. While the wailing sounds of imagined pain surged through the room,

I kept thanking God for His triumph over darkness.

The third step, Embracing and Understanding, offered only pagan myths and hollow affirmations as solutions to life's pain. A story about the Japanese sun goddess ended with a futile solution to fear: a mirror for gazing at one's own glory.

Rapture and Transformation, the fourth step in the journey toward "the Sacred feminine, Source of our being," was led by Andrew Harvey, a guru to Westerners seeking Eastern mystical experience. Like most contemporary pagans, he blends beliefs and practices from many earth-centered traditions to create his own expression. His personal mix of eastern meditation, western witchcraft, Sufi mysteries, and Jungian psychology seemed to have won him the status of a revered master.

Mocking the Ten Commandments, he listed "Ten Rather Firm Suggestions." The ninth suggestion typifies the sensual focus of contemporary paganism:

TEN RATHER FIRM SUGGESTIONS:

1. Adore me . . . the Mother. Know that I, the Mother, am immanent and transcendent.
2. Adore every sentient [feeling] being . . . with my total tenderness.
3. Dare to adore yourself as my divine child.
4. Know . . . that nature is the sacred body of my sacred life.
5. Know that my love is eternally active. . . .
6. Shine to all four directions.
7. Dissolve all social barriers between sects and religions.
8. Dissolve all barriers between the . . . sacred and the profane.
9. Discover and cultivate sacred Eros in all its ecstatic connections.

10. Know that I can be contacted anywhere at anytime through one sacred syllable: "Ma." No intermediary needed.

Since Harvey communicates directly with pagan spirits, he receives the mystical kinds of messages that fuel today's spiritual rebellion.

Recently, the "Divine Mother," told him, "Everything will be transformed when you know and see me. . . . I have willed the end of homophobia. I have willed the end of reason. I have willed the end of denial of the sanctity of the body. . . . I have willed . . . the end of the exploitation of nature. For I have willed a garden. . . ."

The Sacred Feminine Conference would continue for two more days at a local Unitarian church, but I had seen enough. Driving home, I thanked my Lord for His victory over occult deities and the forces they represent. He alone can bring a renaissance of truth and light into this spreading darkness.

Looking Ahead

Will there be a garden under the reign of the goddess? Harvey's "Divine Mother" said there would, but *who* is she?

She whispers mysteries the world longs to hear, but what makes her myths so believable — even to church leaders? What happens to women seduced by her promises, and where is she taking our children? What happens to nations that turn to "other gods" and values? What happens to Christians in such cultures?

These and other crucial questions will be explored in the rest of this book. In each chapter we will look at a phrase in the prayer Jesus taught His disciples, then show how it is turned upside-down by the feminist spirituality movement.

Following the outline of the following prayer, we will explore the main myths fueling today's pagan revival, and the major truths that lead us back to intimacy with God.

Praying to God	Affirming the Goddess
Our Father in heaven	Our Mother, the Earth
Holy is Your Name	Sacred and perfect am I
Your Kingdom Come	My vision come
Your will be done	My will be done
Give us . . . daily bread	Don't give . . . I own . . .
Forgive us . . . as we forgive	I choose to forgive — or curse
Lead us not into temptation	Temptation? I form my own values
Deliver us from evil	There is no sin or evil
For Yours is the . . . power	Mine is the power
. . . forever!	Nothing is permanent or absolute.

To a woman seeking new directions, feminine faces for God, and a better image of herself, the path to feminist spirituality may look bright with promise. Yet, like Peggy, many find themselves in the depths of spiritual confusion and loneliness once the initial euphoria fades. Some are trapped in downward spiritual spiral they can't escape. All too late, they see that feminist promises bring conflict instead of love and confusion instead of peace.

A worldwide sisterhood of angry, militant feminists is rising to power. The United Nations World Conference on Women in Beijing gave a glimpse of its influence. It left its leaders with marching orders designed to revolutionize our schools, homes, churches and culture. If the feminist movement gains what it demands, no one will escape its global influence. American Christians will face the kind of hatred that drove persecuted masses to our borders, but there would be no place to hide outside of Christ.

As we look at these changes in the light of God's Word, He helps us understand the crisis and prepare for the coming conflict. If we trust Him, He will not only keep us spiritually safe during our journey, He will show us a joy and victory only possible for those who have dared to face reality, refused to compromise, and set their mind to trust the Shepherd.

Endnotes

[1] The Re-Imagining Conference in Minneapolis, Minnesota, November 4–7, 1993, *NEWS*, January 7, 1994.

[2] Ambrose Evans-Pritchard, "Every Witch Way to the Goddess," *The Sunday Telegraph,* October 17, 1993.

[3] Re-Imagining Conference, tape 12-1, side B.

[4] Mark Tooley, "Great Goddess Almighty," *Heterodoxy* (October 1995); p. 6.

[5] In *The Aquarian Conspiracy*, New Age leader Marilyn Ferguson wrote: "Of the Aquarian Conspirators surveyed, more were involved in education than in any other single category of work. They were teachers, administrators, policymakers, educational psychologists..." (page 280). My own observations confirm Ms. Ferguson's assertion. Since I wrote *Under the Spell of Mother Earth*, I have received reports from parents across the country documenting the use of Native American or Wiccan rituals by enthusiastic female teachers as part of environmental, global, or multicultural education.

[6] Mary Hunt is co-director of WATER (Women's Alliance for Theology, Ethics, and Ritual) in Silver Springs, Maryland. "Mary Hunt: Goddess Equals Diversity, Pluralism," *Religious News Service*, July 16, 1993.

Chapter 2

Holy Is Your Name,
or
Sacred and Perfect Am I?

❧

I found god in myself, and I loved her, I loved her fiercely. (Ntozake Shange quoted at the Re-imagining Conference)

I don't think we need a theory of atonement at all. . . . I don't think we need folks hanging on crosses and blood dripping and weird stuff.[1] (Rev. Delores Williams, speaking at the Re-imagining Conference)

Priests have violated My law and profaned My holy things; they have not distinguished between the holy and unholy. . . . I am profaned among them. (Ezek. 21:26)

❧

The Feminine Face of God? Stopped by the suggestive title, I pulled the book from the shelf in our local bookstore, and pondered the subtitle: "The Unfolding of the Sacred in Women." *What did that mean?*

I turned it over and read the endorsement on the back.

"This is a book that invites women to define for themselves what is sacred. . . ."

Women, not God, would define what is sacred? Then "the sacred" could mean anything! Or could it?

Hoping to learn more about the spiritual quests of women, I brought the book to the sales counter. While waiting, I scanned some of the miniature books on display. A tiny book titled *Oneness* explained that prayer and meditation "will center us . . . so that we can recognize the divine within ourselves."[2] Page after tiny page emphasized a pantheistic oneness of all beliefs — a unity that assumes that all people are joined to the same "Universal Consciousness" or sacred source of life. *No need for the cross if each person is already made sacred through union with a cosmic god,* I thought as I put it back.

I picked up another book, Thomas Merton's *Ways of the Christian Mystics,* and flipped through its miniature pages. Published by Shambala, a prolific producer of occult literature, it told of a "sacred journey" with "origins in prehistoric religious cultures and myths."[3]

Myths instead of truth? I felt sad but not surprised. Few spiritual teachers have done more to blend biblical sacredness with eastern mysticism than Merton, the popular Catholic author who died in Asia searching the depths of Tibetan Buddhism. Yet thousands of Christian women search his books for simple paths to intimacy with God.

Merton's little book echoes the theme of universal oneness. "Our pilgrimage," he wrote, "is to the stranger who is Christ our fellow-pilgrim and our brother."[4] He suggests some of the potential strangers: the Inca, Maya, or aborigine who is "no other than ourselves, which is the same as saying that we find Christ in him." *No matter which gods he or she worships?*

"Yes," cry a chorus of contemporary voices. Respected guides such as Thomas Merton have opened the door to countless spiritual alternatives by tearing down the biblical separation between the holiness of God and the unholy spirits behind pagan religions. It may sound compassionate to blend the two and trust that both paths lead to the same destination, but it's not true. They are incompatible. God withdrew His presence from His holy temple back in Old Testament days. His people had profaned it by worshiping their Canaanite gods and goddesses inside its walls. Having lost God's blessing and protection, the nation that had been the envy of its neighbors was soon destroyed by immorality, greed, famine, and war.

Today's search for meaning is nudging our entire nation along the same self-destructive paths, for human nature hasn't changed. It still pulls us toward self-made gods that model all the sensual thrills and unrestrained lifestyles we can imagine. So it's not surprising that the ancient goddesses revived by radical feminists some decades ago now captivate women around the world. Those who prefer to keep their Christian identity simply choose deities that sound more biblical. Their best match is Sophia, named after the Greek word for *wisdom*.[5] To early Gnostics, whose self-focused teaching seeped into first century churches, she symbolized holiness and salvation through mystical knowledge, not through Jesus Christ.

You may remember that Sophia starred at the controversial Re-Imagining Conference in Minnesota. She also seduces women through more intimate neo-pagan neighborhood "Circles" that throw the biblical cross to the winds. One such Sophia Circle was advertised in a small newspaper someone sent me. "Women's ritual group drawing from a variety of spiritual traditions welcomes new members for monthly gatherings," it beckoned. "If interested, call Karen."[6]

I called Karen. "Are you connected in any way with the 1993 Re-imagining Conference in Minnesota?" I asked. She assured me they were not. A week later I joined more than a dozen women at a local Catholic retreat center.

The Sophia Circle

Each woman arrived with a gift for her favorite goddess. One by one, they laid their sacrifices on the lovely embroidered cloth serving as an altar. Soon the center of the living room floor sparkled with all kinds of natural and personal treasures: multicolored roses, camellias, cala lilies, a family photograph, a can of Heath candy, a treasured book, a tree branch covered with spring leaves. . . .

"Take off your shoes," someone suggested, "this is holy ground."

Holy ground? I couldn't help but think of Moses at the burning bush. He stood on holy ground because God had touched it with His own presence. This meant the opposite.

The women kicked off their shoes and sandals, and formed a ring around the festive, multicolored offerings. With chants, rattles, and a drum, they "cast a circle," creating a "sacred space" for experiencing the presence and power of the goddess. In turn, they invoked the spirits of the North, East, South, and West.

Karen pulled out some matches and lit a foot-long sage wand, the kind neo-pagans make from sweet-smelling herbs. She turned to the woman on her left, waved the smoldering wand around her body, over her head, down one side, up the other side, enveloping her in the fragrant smoke that soon spread like incense through the room. She did the same with the next woman, and the next . . . all around the circle.

American Indians use the aromatic smoke from sage or sweetgrass to purify themselves, I thought. *Did these women think the smoke would cleanse them spiritually?*

No one offered an explanation. The cleansing ritual was obviously familiar to them.

Karen filled a crystal goblet with apple juice and passed it around the ring of women. Each person sipped, wiped the spot with a napkin, and handed it to the next person. When the communion-like cup had completed the circle, a grandmotherly woman led a healing exercise using a blend of visualization and kinesthesiology. "Release the child within," she said. "Rub your forehead. Remember the chakras and rub the third eye in your forehead. . . . Rub your chest. . . ."

The chakras of Kundalini yoga — a sexual ritual that joins the sacred female force to the male force? Watching from a few feet back, I repeated the words Jesus gave His disciples, *"Our Father in heaven, holy is your name. . . ."*

An "empowering" ritual followed the healing exercise. Clapping hands, tapping their knees, and clicking their fingers to a steady beat, they declared their wants to the unseen goddess. "Strength!" one shouted. Others called for peace, unity, good relationship with daughters, healing. . . . "Ye-ah, ye-ah, ye-ah, ye-ah," they chanted after each assertion.

The ceremony ended the way it began: with drums, rattles, prayer to Sophia, and a ritual dance to the spirits of the four directions. Liz, one of the leaders, began pulling the greenery off the make-shift altar. "How did this group get started?" I asked her.

"I helped start it four years ago," she answered.

"Why?"

"I wanted to enable women to cope." She looked at me and smiled. "I wouldn't use that word now. An enabler used to be a good word. Now it's not."

"Strange how words and values change, isn't it? Makes it hard to know how to communicate with people — unless you know them really well."

She nodded.

"Are most of the women here Catholic?"

"Some are, but they come from different backgrounds. Some used to go to church. Others never did. But they all feel a need for spirituality. They just don't feel comfortable in traditional churches."

"Did those churches hurt or disappoint them?"

"They hurt me. I didn't feel I belonged there. They told

me that men were made in the image of God, but women were not. Since Jesus was a man, only men could follow in His footsteps. I wasn't allowed to express who I really am."

I wanted to tell her how free I felt to be myself and express His life in my church, but hesitated. It wasn't the right time. So I changed the subject and prayed for an opportunity to talk again. "How often do you meet?" I asked.

"Every month. And we try to meet as close to the full moon as possible."

"Why is the full moon so important?" I thought I knew the answer, but I wanted to hear it from her.

"The moon represents the face of the goddess," she answered. "When the moon is waxing, we call it the maiden. The full moon is the matron, and the waning moon is the crone."

I almost said, "But isn't that witchcraft?" Just then, she turned to someone waiting to talk.

"O God," I whispered, *"These are such empty substitutes for your great power!"*

The full face of the moon lit the path as I walked back to my car. It reminded me of Barbra Streisand's song, "Woman in the Moon," which helped Shawntell Smith win the 1995 Miss America contest. Its words fit these women who loved the goddess. "I was raised in a no-you-don't world," sang Streisand, dramatizing her disdain for traditional values. But "You and I are changing our tune. We're learning new rhythms from that woman — I said, the woman in the moon. . . . O ye-ah, ye-ah!"[7]

Women everywhere are learning to follow the rhythms of "that woman in the moon." Despising God's standard for holiness, they create their own. To feminist theologian Mary Daly that "involves breaking taboos," being "wicked women," "riding the rhythms of . . . rage," and "seeking sister vibrations."[8] For "sisterhood means revolution"[9] — a rising revolt against biblical beliefs and values that is proving the timeless allure of pagan spirituality.

In November 1993, that allure drew over 2,000 women from mainline churches in 49 states and 27 countries[10] to Minneapolis, Minnesota. They came together to re-imagine Jesus, themselves, their sexuality, and their world. Like their spiritual sisters in local circles, they wanted a new god with a feminine face. They called "her" Sophia — or any other name that fit their visions. Funded in part by their Presbyterian, Methodist, Baptist, and Lutheran denominations,[11] the four-day conference sent shockwaves across our nation that are still shaking the Church.

Susan Cyre, a concerned Christian and a Presbyterian reporter, documented what happened and shared her observations with me. The following quotes from her tapes and transcripts show how feminist beliefs are changing our churches and neighborhoods, as well as cultures around the world.

Re-imagining God

"We invoke Sophia, Divine Wisdom," prayed over 2,000 women and about 60 men at the opening ceremony to the Re-imagining conference in Minneapolis. "Let her speak and bless us throughout these days."[12]

Who is this divine Sophia? To some, she is merely a personified expression of the Greek word for wisdom, but at this conference she could be anything and everything: creator, healer, lover, power, passion, sex, impersonal force, global mind. The program book simply identified her as "the place in you where the entire universe resides."[13]

The new theology would be grounded in personal experience, not the Bible. Women would finally be free to express their feelings. They would "name" their "own truth," "imagine" their own god, and "dream wildly about" their own sacred identity.[14] They would not be told what to believe (though they would be exposed to plenty of choices). The inspiration would come from within — that sacred part of self where the goddess, who *is* "the entire universe," resides.

Like most neo-pagan celebrations, the conference began by "Making Holy Space" to the beat of Native American drums. "The drum is feminine," explained the program, "and the drumbeat is the heartbeat of the earth. . . . The heart of mother earth indeed beats with our own as one."[15]

"As one we sing to her our sacred song," sang the women over and over, affirming their interfaith oneness. "As one we touch her, as one we heal her, her heart beats with our own as one."

Seated in intimate Native American "talking circles" around the tables, the assembly imagined the faces of god. "What does your god sound like, taste like, look like?" they asked each other, while the sounds of a water drum throbbed in the air. "Tell each other. . . . Re-imagine your God. Name! Tell! Image!"[16]

To help the women visualize their own goddess, the leaders suggested a medley of exotic images. Sophia might be her "Christian" name, but the options were boundless: Mystery, Lover, Earth Mother, Spirit Woman, She Who Is, Cosmic Maxim, Transforming Laughter, Womb of Creation, Yin Yang, Unknown God.

"Bring every name, overlooking none,"[17] sang the assembly.

"They would move from the familiar to the bizarre," said Susan Cyre. "They would start with traditional names like Adonai and Father, and pretty soon they would be into Yin and Yang and Joyful Darkness, using the familiar as a springboard, then just changing one or two words and moving into the unfamiliar. There was enough of the familiar to disarm them, but it was twisted."[18]

Each speaker brought new images that fed the imagination. "If we cannot imagine Jesus as a tree, as a river, as wind, and as rain, we are doomed together,"[19] warned Kwok Pui-Lan, a Chinese theologian.

"The three goddesses I want to share with you are Kali [Hindu], Kwan-in [Buddhist], and Enna [Phillipines] . . . my new trinity,"[20] said Chung Hyun Kyung, a Korean theologian educated at Union Theological Seminary. She explained why:

> I came from . . . a Shamanist, Buddhist, Confucian, Taoist, and Christian tradition. . . . When I look at our history of religion, we have more than 5,000 years of Shamanism, more than 2,000 years of Taoism, and almost 2,000 years of Buddhism, and 700 years of Confucianism and only 100 years of Protestantism in Korea. Therefore, whenever I go to temples . . . and look at Buddha, I feel so young . . . Buddha died in his eighties and Jesus died when he was 33. Maybe . . . Jesus should be called, "Too young to understand."[21]

Her mockery sent ripples of laughter through the room.

"I'm not just doing inter-religious dialogue with Buddhist, Confucionists, and Taoist," Kyung continued, "because all of them are within me. As my friend introduced me, I feel like my bowel is Shamanist, my heart is Buddhist, my right brain is Confucianist, and my left brain is Christian. . . . I call it a family of gods and . . . they are together."[22]

This kind of spiritual compromise is anything but new. Back in Old Testament days, God's people would burn incense to their idols in "sacred groves" one day, then worship God the next. He often warned them to shun "other gods," for He knew fear and oppression would follow occult worship. But the people refused to listen.

To speed the shift from the biblical God to new feminist images, the conference organizers had planned rituals that would clash with Christianity and support neo-paganism. The women prayed Native American prayers, used ritual tobacco, blessed "rainsticks", and joined in Hawaiian chants and Zulu songs. Led by Indian feminist Aruna Gnanadason, they anointed themselves with red dots on the forehead to celebrate "the divine in each other"[23] and to protest the oppression brought to India by Christian missionaries.

Any spiritual expression was welcomed — except biblical Christianity. "In a global context where violence and the use of force have become the norm," said Aruna Gnanadason, "the violence that the Cross symbolizes and the patriarchal image of an almighty invincible Father God needs to be challenged and reconstructed."[24]

Unholy Visions

Out of the ashes of the old ways would spring the new holistic church that worships "god herself," gives "honor to every world religion," and agrees that "everything that lives is holy." So said Virginia Mollenkott, a lesbian feminist who helped the National Council of Churches write an inclusive language lectionary. She suggested three models for this new church: the "Women-church within the Roman Catholic communion, the Evangelical and Ecumenical Women's Caucus, and the Universal Fellowship of Metropolitan Community Churches [which] includes Catholics, Orthodox, Protestants, Mormons, Charismatic, and Wiccans [witches]." This new church would be formed by a "liberated minority in every denominations."[25]

Women liberated to what? Would this new church *really* offer the freedom women want? Or would they be forced to submit to new uncompromising guidelines and social controls?

Kathy Kersten, a lawyer and a Lutheran reporter, wondered. Like many others who have observed the rise of feminism, she had noticed a harsh militancy that seemed more inflexible than anything she had seen in the traditional church. For example, the leaders of the Re-Imagining conference had stationed 50 monitors to stand guard at all times to make sure each attendee participated in every New Age ritual and consciousness-raising exercise with proper enthusiasm.

"Participants had initially been told that joining in was voluntary," said Kathy Kersten, "but the conference news-letter advised: 'Participation is intended for ALL in the gathering — rituals are not spectator events. . . . We thank you all for your full, active, conscious participation. May Sophia continue to bless your pilgrimage.' "[26]

Though the women were told to discover "their own truth" and god, their spiritual mentors had already written the guidelines. Naturally, some traits of the re-imagined gods were open to individual preference. The new deities *could* be personal and loving (like Jesus) or be impersonal but empowering (like the cosmic force or *ch'i* energy). But they had to be *immanent* (everywhere and in all) like the Native American Great Spirit and other pantheistic deities. They could not be *transcendent* (higher and greater than they) or selective (choosing to save some and not others) like the biblical God. They had to mirror each woman's own self, not some higher revelation. In other words, Jesus Christ was ruled out.

"New gods arise when they are needed,"[27] the women were told. Since the need seemed urgent, Chung Hyun Kyung suggested one of her favorite images as an option:

> We believe that this life-giving energy came from god and it is everywhere. It is in the sun, in the ocean, it is from the ground, and it is from the trees. . . . If you feel very tired and you feel you don't have any energy to give, what you do is sit in silence, maybe you go to big tree and ask . . . "give me some of your life energy." Or you ask the sun to give you some life energy.[28]

Spiritual energy in the sun, ocean, ground, and trees? If you watched Disney's box-office hit *Pocahontas* or read *The Celestine Prophecy,* James Redfield's top-selling manual for spiritual evolution toward universal peace and oneness, you have already been exposed to this spirituality. It's all around us. We see it in martial arts, yoga, holistic massages, and the slow-moving Tai Chi exercises. The same pantheistic message echoes through popular books, magazines, television, the media, and schools. Everything is sacred, because everything is connected to the life of the goddess or universal force. Therefore everything is good — except the old biblical views of holiness.

To establish the new beliefs, Chung Hyun Kyung encouraged daily practice. She taught the women to lift their arms, feel the sacred energy that permeates everything, and receive it into themselves. "If you practice it very, very much every day," she said, "you can really start to feel the energy of people so you just intuitive[ly] know what you need to do for your neighbor."[29]

The leaders of the Re-Imagining conference knew that biblical truth could not co-exist with this seductive blend of Eastern and Western mysticism. Faith in a sacred self, spirit-filled trees, or a cosmic energy source tends to nullify any conscious need for the Cross. As Delores Williams, professor at Union Theological Seminary told the group, "I don't think we need folks hanging on crosses and blood dripping and weird stuff."[30]

She simply didn't understand. Having immersed her mind in feminist theology, she had lost sight both of God's goodness and humanity's deepest need.

"Be Holy as I Am Holy"

God said that because He loves us. He, who understands us far better than we know ourselves, wants to protect us, not control us. Unlike people who idealize paganism, He sees the pain and anger that comes with counterfeit spirituality. His warnings were meant to keep us safe, not to burden us with heavy legal requirements.

Many women today refuse to believe that. They link holiness to an "impossible" standard, and they feel frustrated. They have seen what legalism can do to women, and they are angry. They feel rejected by church leaders, and they want alternatives. They feel oppressed by husbands who demand submission but refuse to follow God's wise counsel ("Love your wives as Christ loved the Church"), and they want out.

The reason for these failures is obvious: our imperfect human nature. None of us can be "righteous" (do the right thing or live a holy life) unless we allow Jesus to do it in us. *Imagining* God can't produce holiness, and *imitating* Him will only produce a shallow substitute for the real thing. Faith in a "sacred self" — the heart of the radical feminist doctrines — not only fails to make us holy, it drives us further away from the One who can.

Our Maker knows this well. To free us from the bondage of our own sinful nature, He offers us the Cross where He gave His life. To conform us to His character, He offers us His holy life. Some call this amazing bargain the exchanged life: I give Him my life and He gives me His. His strength and holiness for my sins and failures. First Corinthians 5:21 sums it up: "God made Him who had no sin to be sin for us, so that in Him we might become the righteousness of God."

In stark contrast to feminist accusations, He came not to burden us with rules, but to heal the brokenhearted, to proclaim liberty to the captives, and the opening of the prison to *those who are* bound . . . to comfort all who mourn . . . to give them beauty for ashes, the oil of joy for mourning, the garment of praise for the spirit of heaviness (see Isa. 61:1–3).

Women who seek God in their mirror will never see this kind of love or understand His holiness. Nor will those who re-write God's Word to fit their wants. For the spiritual power behind their new-found gods has blinded their eyes to truth, so they cannot see "the light of the gospel of the glory of Christ" (2 Cor. 4:3–6).

Instead, they plan to quench that light, for it upsets their visions. "The light has come into the world," explained

John, "and men loved darkness rather than light, because their deeds were evil. For everyone practicing evil hates the light and does not come to the light, lest his deeds should be exposed" (John 3:19–21).

Turning truth upside-down, theologian Mary Daly offers a solution for this timeless conflict. "I propose that Christianity itself should be castrated by cutting away the products of supermale arrogance: the myths of sin and salvation," she wrote in *Beyond God the Father.* "Rather than a fall *from* the sacred, the fall now initiated by women becomes a fall *into* the sacred and therefore into freedom."[31]

At the Re-Imagining conference, Cuban theologian Ada Maria Isasi-Diaz showed the way to communicate this distorted vision. She called for "a new Pentecost" — a new way of seeing reality. "We need to develop . . . a *lens* . . . to understand that the way things are is not natural," she explained, "[so that] we can change them radically. . . . We have to move from being liberals to being radicals."[32]

Two Opposing Paradigms

Ms. Isasi-Diaz was talking about a *paradigm shift.* Her "lens" is like a mental filter that narrows her vision of the world to fit her new convictions. Like the popular Native American fetish called a *dreamcatcher,* it permits only ideas that support the "right" beliefs to settle in the mind. It rules out all contrary ideas. This new view of "reality" looks something like this:

• Everything is connected to the same sacred source, goddess, or universal mind.

• Therefore everything is naturally sacred and good.

• Therefore insights from my "inner self" are true and the biblical view of sin is merely a patriarchal club for controlling women.

• Therefore the Church, the cross, and male authority obstruct the vision of a sacred oneness that will save the world.

   • Therefore we must re-imagine God, ourselves, the Bible, and our world.
   • Therefore biblical Christianity doesn't fit.

To establish this new paradigm, the old biblical "lens" must be dropped or altered. You saw two of the strategies for change: re-imagine God and mix biblical words with pagan beliefs until Christianity loses its uniqueness. Both lead to a seductive blend that sounds Christian but is nothing like Christianity.

The paradigm you choose determines what you will see, for the filter works both ways. Those who wear the feminist lens cannot understand why Christians love their God. Nor can they understand why Jesus had to die to save us from bondage to sin. Such love makes no sense! It can't, for God only shows the depths of His love to those who are part of His family. As He told us long ago:

> Eye has not seen, nor ear heard, nor have entered into the heart of man the things which God has prepared for those who love Him. But God has revealed *them* to us through His Spirit. For the Spirit searches all things, yes, the deep things of God. . . . Now we have received, not the spirit of the world, but the Spirit who is from God, that we might know the things that have been freely given to us by God. . . . But the *natural man does not receive the things of the Spirit of God, for they are foolishness to him; nor can he know them, because they are spiritually discerned* (1 Cor. 2:9–15).

If you have received God's Spirit, He will show you things others can't see. You will understand the difference between His holiness and unholy counterfeits. You will see the greatness of God's compassion, and you will shudder at the natural consequences of today's popular deceptions. You will see, wherever you turn, why the words written by the prophet Isaiah over 2000 years ago still fit today:

> Woe to those who call evil good and good evil, who put darkness for light and light for darkness. . . . Woe to those who are *wise in their own eyes* and prudent *[clever]* in their own sight (Isa. 5:20–21).

Those who are "wise in their own eyes" belong in the new paradigm, which is almost as old as time. From the beginning, pagan substitutes for God's holy presence have dulled human discernment and brought social disaster — a natural sequence we'll look at in later chapters. Each time, God's *good* gifts were twisted into deceptive promises or rejected as dangerous obstacles to imagined peace.

To guard us against the blinding force of this hoax, God gave us a sacred shelter — a place of safety — one far different from the neo-pagan's *sacred space*. Called an "armor" in Ephesians 6:10–18, it outlines the truths needed to expose and counter all the main pagan deceptions. But it's more than that. When we choose to believe the truth about God, accept His provision for our sin, and receive His righteous life, He not only fills us with His Holy Spirit, He also covers us with himself (Gal. 3:27 and Rom. 13:14).

To live each day in the safety of His protection, "put on the Lord Jesus Christ," His holy life. One way is to affirm the truths and promises of the armor. The first and main truth looks at God as He has revealed himself, for the most dangerous deceptions are counterfeit gods and unholy distortions of His holy character. Remember the first commandment: "You shall have no other gods. . . ."

The Christian paradigm shows holiness from a biblical perspective; the other shows counterfeit sacredness from a neo-pagan perspective. Notice the difference. Learn the

Scriptures. Think, whisper, or speak God's Word back to Him whenever you face a spiritual or moral battle. Then trust Him to provide the wisdom and strength needed for victory. It's exciting! I couldn't go the places He sends me if I didn't wear this armor.

THE ARMOR OF GOD		
Each Piece Put on:	*Old (Christian) Paradigm* Know and affirm:	*New (pagan) Paradigm* Recognize and resist:
Belt of TRUTH	His sovereignty, love, wisdom, and holiness (Deut. 4:39; Ps. 18:1–3)	Pantheistic, monistic, polytheistic gods and goddesses.
Breastplate of RIGHT-EOUSNESS:	Jesus Christ and His blood, which cleanses us from sin. The cross which frees us from bondage to selfish nature (Rom. 3:23–24, 6:23; Gal. 2:20–21; 1 John 1:9).	The natural goodness connectedness, and sacredness of all life.
Sandals of PEACE	Our peace through our union and on-going relationship with Jesus Christ (Eph. 2:14; John 14:27, 16:33).	Peace through occult practices and union with a cosmic force or nature spirits.

Shield of FAITH	Our continual trust in God, His Word, and His promises (Rom. 4:18–21; Heb. 11:1; 1 Pet. 1:6–7).	Trust in self, inner wisdom, dreams, visions, gods, goddesses, cosmic force, coincidences, etc.
Helmet of SALVATION	God's promises of daily and eternal salvation in Jesus Christ (Ps. 16, 23; 2 Pet. 1:3–4; 1 John 3:1–3).	Evolving spiritually by growing in consciousness and staying tuned to the cosmic mind.[33]
Sword of the Spirit, His WORD	The power of God's Word to counter deception and triumph over spiritual foes (Heb. 4:12; 2 Cor. 10:3–5; 1 Pet. 3:15).	The power of thoughts, words, and affirmations to change reality and direct spiritual forces.

The two paradigms mix like oil and water. So do the two views of holiness: God's revelation of *him*self and the feminist new view of *her*self. Later chapters will show what happens when women trust the latter. Keep in mind, this movement is far greater than your church, community, or nation. Its goal is to transform the entire world. Hard to believe? You may be surprised to see how far it has already come.

Endnotes

[1] Re-Imagining Conference, tape 3-2, Side B. Delores Williams is associate professor of theology and culture at Union Theological Seminary in NY. Program booklet p. 56.

[2] Jeffrey Moses, *Oneness* (New York, NY: Fawcett Columbine, 1989), p. 109.

[3] Thomas Merton, *Ways of the Christian Mystic* (Boston, MA: Shambala, 1994), p. 1.

[4] Ibid., p. 49–50.

[5] Chokmah [khok-maw'], the Hebrew word for wisdom, skill, shrewdness, prudence, and wits, is used 141 times in the Old Testament. Since it is a feminine gender word which is personified in Proverbs 8:1 and 12, feminists argue that it refers to a feminine deity separate from God or a feminized version of God. This conclusion, based on this small poetic portion of Scripture, clashes with all the rest of Scripture which points to one God in three persons — God the Father, Jesus Christ the Son, and the Holy Spirit.

[6] *Catholic Women's Network*, March/April 1995.

[7] *A Star is Born* (Producer: Barbra Streisand), Warner Brothers, 1976.

[8] Mary Daly, *Beyond God the Father* (Boston, MA: Beacon Press, 1973), p. xxv.

[9] Ibid., p. 59.

[10] Katherine Kersten, "God in Your Mirror?" *The Lutheran Commentator* (May/June 1994), p. 1.

[11] All funders were listed in the Re-Imagining program booklet, p. 66. The largest single contributor was the Presbyterian Church (USA) which gave $66,000 from their Bicentennial Fund. An additional $20,000 covered staff expenses to attend and scholarships for Presbyterians. Other contributors included the ELCA (Lutheran), Baptists, and United Methodist.

[12] Ibid., p. 19.

[13] Kersten, "God in Your Mirror," p. 2.

[14] Re-Imagining conference program book, p. 11, tape 1-1, side A.

[15] Ibid., p. 9.

[16] Re-Imagining conference, tape 2-1, side A.

[17] Re-Imagining program book, p. 13, also tape 1-1, side A.

[18] Telephone conversation with Susan Cyre on Monday, July 24, 1995.

[19] Re-Imagining conference, tape 3-2, side A.

[20] Ibid., tape 2-2, side A.

[21] Ibid.

[22] Ibid.

[23] "Anointing with Red Dot Ritual," Friday plenary, tape 2-1, side A. "Rainsticks" are mentioned in program book, p. 30.

[24]Susan Cyre, "Women's Conference Re-imagines New God," *Rutherford*, August 1994, p. 19.

[25]Re-Imagining Conference, tape 11-2, side A.

[26]Kersten, p. 7.

[27]Josephine Johnson. Quoted in a list of statements about God and spirituality read to the assembly. Conference tape 2-1, side A.

[28]Re-Imagining conference, Saturday plenary, tape 7-1, side A.

[29]Ibid.

[30]Re-Imagining conference, tape 3-2, side B.

[31]Mary Daly, *Beyond God the Father* (Boston, MA: Beacon Press, 1973), p. 67.

[32]Ibid., tape 5-1, side A.

[33]This will be explained in chapter 10.

Chapter 3

Your Kingdom Come,
or
My Kingdom Come?

∽

God is going to change. We women . . . will change the world so much that He won't fit anymore. (Naomi Goldenberg in *Changing of the Gods: Feminism and the End of Traditional Religions*)[1]

While women sleep the earth shall sleep. But listen! We are waking up and rising, and soon our sister will know her strength. The earth-moving day is here. (Alla Bozarth-Campbell, Episcopal priest, 1974)[2]

Our kingdom is our life, and our life is our kingdom. We are all meant to rule from a glorious place. (Marianne Williamson, *A Woman's Worth*)[3]

My Kingdom is not of this world. (John 18:36; Jesus speaking to His friends)

∽

When Pat was little, Jesus seemed so near. But that feeling of closeness faded when she reached high school. It wasn't that she lacked interest; she just had so many other things to explore: Egyptian and Mayan mythology, ancient mystery religions, Greek and Roman goddesses. She read books about mysterious people like Edgar Cayce, the "sleeping prophet" who could "see" and heal the sick from miles away. Miracles like that never happened in her church! But out there, in those mystical realms, there seemed to be something more — a dimension of spiritual power and knowledge beyond what the Bible taught. The possibilities fascinated her.

College entrance opened new doors to spiritual discoveries. Each of the world's religions seemed to have something to offer, and the options were endless. How could she pick and choose what fit her needs — and what could be mixed with her Christian faith? Each new path deepened her curiosity.

In 1980 her mother died. The ache and loneliness that followed the funeral stirred a longing for the loving comfort Pat had known long ago with Jesus. That longing drew her home to her widowed father — and back to church.

But the magical forces Pat had studied in her college days still tugged at her heart. She couldn't forget Edgar Cayce. His form of spiritism and re-incarnation seemed so compassionate and Christ-like. So did Buddhism. Perhaps her old biblical boundaries were too narrow. After all, Cayce really did receive supernatural insights from the spirit world. Maybe she could try to make the same kind of contacts — even talk with her mother. Or — perhaps her mother would return in some other body? Either way, they would find each other.

One night she heard an audible voice speak her name. "Pat," it said. She was standing outside near a street lamp waiting for a bus. "Pat!" It said it again and again. Something compelled her to turn her head toward the north, and suddenly she saw a ball of bright light flash along the high wires above the sidewalk. It shot across the street and shattered into many small lights.

What kind of "sign and wonder" was this? Could it have been Jesus? Pat felt more frightened than thrilled. But the spirit that had spoken to her stayed. It kept affirming her, told her she was special, and did nothing else that was scary — at least not for a while.

A few months later, Pat found a sick cat. She knelt down to pet it and felt a large lump on his chest. Urged by her new spirit, she put her hands over the lump. "Heal!" she commanded several times. The next day the cat walked into her yard. She felt its chest. The lump was gone. This was a miracle! Wow! She did it! The healing had come through her hands. She felt wonderful, powerful . . . as if she could cure anyone, anytime. She named the cat "Angel."

She went inside and tried her healing power on her own cancer-ridden little cat, Toby. But it didn't work. Toby died. Pat felt sad and confused.

The voice began to direct her spiritual training. It prompted her to pick up a New Age magazine, to focus on a name that "shone out" from one of its pages, and to contact one of several people who would help "enlighten" her. Soon her spiritual teachers were opening doors into that vast twilight world of hypnotic visions and occult dreams. She began to "see" fairies, witch covens, pyramids, and the glories of the mythical Atlantis.

In one of her visions she was part of a mystical ceremony. Someone in a long robe gave her grain to eat and wine to drink, a cloak to wear, and a crown of flowers for her head. People from all kinds of cultures were "praying to some deity and placing their gifts on a table illumined by a bright light." Angels, "handsome creatures with wings," flew in and out.

"It was an initiation to something," explained her spiritual guide later.

To heal her from what her guide called her "traumatic past lives," he taught her to alter her consciousness through meditation and self-hypnosis. One such meditation opened her "eyes" to a spiritual being seated on a crystal throne atop a mountain. During another vision a beautiful woman came toward her with arms wide open. Frightened, Pat pulled back, and the spirit woman turned away from her. Could her fear have angered the spirit woman? Pat wondered — and worried.

Other people introduced her to the powers of crystals and Native American shamanism. She let her hair grow long and became a vegetarian. Meditating with a group of friends inside a circle of stones one night, she saw signs in the sky: some star-shaped clouds and a cross. What did it mean? She felt confused. The intense sense of peace with the universe — a feeling she so often enjoyed in the beginning — became rare and fleeting.

The spirit inside Pat seemed increasingly possessive. Friendly and affirming at first, it now governed her every move. The initial voice was joined by other voices that talked to her day and night. They told her when to leave her house, when to cross the street, where to stand on the subway, and what to read. She would call out to God for help, but reading the Scriptures was not an option. The voices refused to let her go near her Bible. She obeyed. What else could she do? Disobedience always intensified the oppression.

She could no longer hold a job, nor sleep peacefully through the night. Her new life of therapy sessions, hypnotic exercises, confusing visions, and harassing voices were taking their toll. Things might go well for a few weeks, then . . . crash. "I guess I would need a hypnosis fix," she explained.

By 1988 Pat knew she needed help — but not from her spirits or New Age friends. She prayed again to the Shepherd she had known as a child. She asked for peace from the voices that oppressed her. And God, who had never stopped loving her, answered her prayer.

Some Christian friends invited her to a seminar on the New Age movement. Pat went, and God began to show her the truth about His love as well as the terrors of the occult. Suddenly she saw the horrendous cruelty behind the seductive spirits that had been fighting for her soul.

"I cried," said Pat, remembering the demons' hatred for the Bible. "I went into shock, and feared for my life."

A few days later a pastor prayed for her deliverance, and she was freed from the demonic spirits that had controlled her life. She accepted Jesus Christ as her Saviour and received the Holy Spirit. Everything became new and different. For the first time in her life, she could understand the Bible.[4] Now God was speaking to her! "You are precious to Me and I love you,"[5] He told her. She knew it was true.

She clung to the promise in John 8:31: "You shall know the truth, and the truth shall set you free." The truth had turned out to be a wonderful friend who not only loved her, He would also keep her safe through the battles ahead. She would need that protection, for the demonic realm doesn't release its victims graciously.

The Two Kingdoms

Pat's transformation is described in Colossians 1:13-14: "He has delivered us from the power of darkness and conveyed us into the kingdom of the Son of His love." Two powers, two rulers. The greater belongs to God, the king who loves His people more than any earthly king ever could. The lesser is ruled by Satan — but only as long as God permits. Both promise peace, love, unity, and power, but only one can satisfy. The other keeps its victims on a tantalizing string: always searching, never finding.

To some, the two may sound similar, but they are as different as night and day. "Love" in the latter is based on sensual feelings and its primary aim is self-love. ("I feel good about myself, therefore I am free to feel loving toward you.") The Re-imagining Conference twisted it further into self-deification.

As rationale for this focus, many women use Jesus' words in Mark 12:31: "You shall love your neighbor as yourself." But Jesus wasn't talking about good feelings toward your neighbors. He meant the kind of love that translates into action: Are you as willing to provide for your neighbor's need as you are for your own? Will you give even if it hurts, and expect nothing in return? Will you trust your Father's love to provide for you when you have nothing left? That's action love, not feeling love, and it can only come from Him, through faith.

Like the meaning of love, the meaning of faith differs from kingdom to kingdom. In God's kingdom, faith is based on His own revelations written in the Bible. Unlike the myths and legends of other spiritual traditions, its meticulous recording of history is consistent with secular history and the findings of modern archeology. Even the droughts and famines mentioned in the Old Testament match the migrations and climatic changes charted by recent scholars. In fact, its historical record and fulfilled prophesies have baffled — even converted — skeptics through the centuries.[6]

Feminist faith in the powers of darkness is based on a person's feelings and experience. In her book *Women at the Well,* Kathleen Fischer summarizes the feminist view:

> Attentiveness to a person's experience is, of course, central. . . . What a feminist perspective adds to this emphasis is belief in the authority of women's experience, confidence that we are engaged in a new encounter with the divine through that experience, and the conviction that it is a norm for the truthfulness of the tradition.[7]

In other words, a woman's experience, not God's own revelation, determines the truthfulness of a belief. If something feels good, sounds loving, and seems empowering, it must be right. Few seekers heed the warning in Jeremiah 17:9: "The heart is deceitful above all things. . . . Who can know it?"

God's truth doesn't matter to those who put their faith in feelings. A leader at the Minnesota Re-imaging Conference described the new faith well: "This is not about making sense at all. It is about honoring a process, an imaginative process, a new way of thinking."[8] Then she led the 2,200 participants in a "scribbling" exercise designed to free them from their old rational ways of thinking, which blocks their freedom to re-imagine God. It also trained them to resist their conscience and inner warnings. Just picking up their crayons and scribbling on the paper tablecloths would start the process. "Make a mark, any mark you want on the paper," urged the leader. "Try again. . . ."

There's nothing wrong with having fun scribbling on tablecloths. But the instructions reached far beyond the simple scribbling time and prepared the women for the pagan suggestions and occult rituals ahead:

> Some of you have this tiny voice inside that says, "This is silly. You can't do this." Well, welcome! That's the inner critic. And we have to deal with that inner critic. . . . So in big letters . . . write down secretly all those words that would keep you from enjoying this. Do it now. . . tear it [the words] out and throw it on the floor. . . . Or take a crayon and scrub them out. Banish them![9]

Remember the story about the emperor's new clothes? The sneaky tailor talked the emperor into buying a phony suit of clothes by telling everyone that the emperor's elegant new outfit would be invisible to fools. Afraid to be called a fool, no one dared admit to seeing nothing but their bare-skinned ruler. On the day of the parade, they all applauded the imaginary suit — all, that is, except one little boy. He hadn't heard the rules (and probably wouldn't have cared), so he shouted to the crowd, "He is wearing nothing at all!"

Like the tailor, Satan makes good use of our imagination. He doesn't hesitate to stir our minds to "see" imagined gods or bright beams of light or ourselves as goddess. He delights in focusing our hearts and prayers on sweet images of angels or a new Jesus rather than on the One who made us. Nothing helps him separate us from God more than today's smorgasbord of spiritual images and forces that promise wisdom and power without accountability.

Millions are ready to listen. Though most of the women at the Re-imagining Conference belonged to mainline churches, they had little resistance to the kinds of occult suggestions that beckoned them. Told to ignore the "inner voice" of their Bible-trained conscience, they imagined "new" realities and embraced new mystical experiences. They left the conference with distorted Scriptures, old truths re-interpreted to affirm feminist visions.

The path chosen by Pat and others headed for the kingdom of God usually lead in the opposite direction. Notice the difference:

BASIS FOR FAITH IN . . .	
GOD'S KINGDOM	THE FEMINIST VISION
The Bible	Imagination (or experience)
Spirit-given insights into truth	Experience (or imagination)
Experiences that affirm Scriptures	Selected Bible verses that affirm the experience

Lacking a firm foundation, feminist faith ranges from simple distortions of biblical truths to the timeless myths of neo-paganism. In between lies every pagan/Christian mixture today's seekers can imagine. Pat's beliefs during her high school years illustrate one of those blends: Since she didn't know the Bible, her limited Christian understanding was stretched to include pagan beliefs and occult experiences.

Such blends soon lose their luster. We know that, not only because Pat experienced it, but because God told us so in His word. "No one can serve two masters," said Jesus. "Either he will hate the one and love the other, or he will be devoted to the one and despise the other" (Matt. 6:24).

The mastermind who rules the kingdom of darkness despises everything that belongs to God. So do his followers. You may have seen some of that hostility in the talks given at the Re-imagining Conference. That anger will surely grow, for those who invoke an occult force — even in the name of God — soon become subject to its cruel ruler. Like his feminist friends, Satan is determined to shut the doors to biblical truth. Church doors are not excluded.

A Strategy for Change

"God is going to change," wrote Naomi Goldenberg in *Changing of the Gods: Feminism and the End of Traditional Religions*. "We women are going to bring an end to God. . . . We will change the world so much that He won't fit in anymore."[10]

Ms. Goldenberg found this thought "most satisfying." She certainly wouldn't miss God. "He never seemed to be relevant to me at all," she said.[11]

Why do so many people who don't know Him or find Him relevant, despise Him with such contagious fervor? Why do they fight so hard to abolish our right to love and follow the biblical God? These are important questions. To resist the wave of change, we need to understand the incredible effort exerted by feminists to alter His image, discredit His followers, and banish His truth even from our churches.

You met Kathleen Fischer earlier in this chapter. In her

book *Women at the Well* she suggests some well-used steps to change. Alone, some steps may sound innocent enough, but together they create a powerful plan for spiritual transformation:

1. Challenge prevailing definitions.
2. Acknowledge the harmful effects of the current sexist society.
3. Fashion "a new creation."
4. Use storytelling to name experience.
5. Bring new meaning to old symbols and texts.
6. Create new rituals.[12]

Her suggestions make a perfect outline for the strategies used at the Re-Imagining Conference. Since many of the conference leaders were also pastors and leaders in their denominations, they give us an inside glimpse at the social revolution that's transforming the Western world.

1. *Challenge prevailing definitions.* It only takes a little ridicule, a few critical questions, some pointed suggestions, and a seductive assortment of old and new myths that clash with traditional biblical views. The conference leaders used all these. Speaking as a Chinese theologian, Kwok Pui-Lan claimed that "the idea that Jesus is the incarnation of God in history was simply irrational, impossible, not understandable. . . . You don't need a Creator,"[13] especially in China. Her argument made sense to those who see reality through the mental filter of the new paradigm.

It makes no sense from a Christian or historical perspective. Remember, China has some of the world's most committed churches. They grow and thrive in the midst of terrible persecution. Modeling life-changing faith, the Chinese Christians love their Lord enough to die for Him. Kwok Pui-Lan and her followers just don't understand how the Holy Spirit works. They can't, because God doesn't reveal His secrets to those who despise His ways.[14]

2. *Acknowledge the harmful effects of the current sex-*

ist society. How do feminists change the nation's social consciousness? You know the answer: forget facts and logic. Instead, use vivid images, feel-good experiences, and outrageous assertions (people won't easily forget them). It only takes a few clever suggestions to create a new perception of a common enemy. Once that enemy is established, public anger can easily be manipulated.

Korean theologian Chung Hyun Kyung did her part well. The "Christian church has been very patriarchal," she said. "That's why we are here together — to destroy this patriarchal idolatry of Christianity."[15]

A Celtic pagan, Anne Primavesi, tried to justify her hatred for the enemy. Ponder her accusations, but remember that God did let Adam and Eve make their own choices. He still gives each of us freedom to choose our own paths. That's why the door to paganism — or back to His kingdom — stands wide open for everyone. Ms. Primavesi twists the truth to fit her goal:

> I too belong to an old tradition, the Celtic tradition. . . . In the creation narratives the focus of attention is on the god who gives commands. . . . There's no appeal allowed, no choice given, their voices are not heard. . . . This god of the male disembodied voice, this god of coercive power over creation . . . is offered in traditional interpretations . . . as the image on which we are to build our relationship.[16]

3. *Fashion a new creation.* New visions demand new foundations. Dr. Elizabeth Bettenhausen, visiting lecturer on ethics at the Harvard Divinity School and former secretary for social concerns of the Lutheran Church in America explained: "We have to re-imagine the doctrine of creation," she said, "because in so much of the traditional orthodox understanding, creation is understood as (the) determined, eternal, unchanging expression of divine will — and that is

downright dangerous for women's lives."[17]

God's divine will dangerous for women? The truth is that the only safe place is in the center of God's will. Those who ignore His ways can never be secure in a culture where people follow their feelings instead of God's unchanging truth.

4. *Bring new meaning to old symbols and texts.* "Way," "truth," and "light," — words vital to Christianity — can be transformed simply by using them in a new context. When Jesus says, "I am the light of the world," He reminds us that He is the living Word that shines into all the world lighting our path and encouraging our hearts.[18]

Now, add the promise Jesus made to His followers in John 14:20: "On that day you will realize that . . . you are in me, and I am in you."

Finally, stir in a cup of New Age mysticism and a spicy touch of sensuality, and you end with a statement like the one by lesbian theologian Mary Hunt:

> A bright warm light, perhaps what New Age people mean when they speak of energy. . . . It is not a light that frightens me, as I am part of it. Nor is it a light that follows me, as I am firmly in its center. And so are you. . . . I see you in the light, your goodness, your erotic power, your commitment to see me in the light as well.[19]

5. *Use storytelling to name experience.* Naming means claiming. Using new paradigm sense, you own what you name. By telling your story, you name and claim your imagined experience. (If this doesn't make sense to you, don't worry. It only fits the new paradigm thinking.)

More "creative" than factual history, home-spun stories feed the imagination and offer an infinite number of illustrations to "confirm" what never really happened. Since good storytellers major in entertainment, not truth, few listeners will question the radical suggestions tucked into their tales. In our times, many find fantasy more believable than facts.

It doesn't matter that the following "story" by Aruna Gnanadason, a theologian from India, seems more like a diatribe than a tale. It made the "right" point, and the audience loved it.

> I chose another medium, and that is the medium of the short story. . . . Once upon a time there was a thing called patriarchy. It was a destructive spirit. It flowed over the earth and it polluted all it touched. . . . And the earth moved on the part of violence, war, poverty, exploitation, and the death of creation. . . .
>
> Then there was an institution called the church. Patriarchy took hold of this thing too. . . .
>
> This is story telling time, re-imagining time. This is dreaming time. . . . Therefore, the story goes on with an ending that can happen. The feminine spirit was not going to rest till life became more bearable for all. She moved women to speak out and take a creative lead in bringing change. . . .
>
> In a global context where violence and the use of force have become the norm, the violence that the cross symbolizes and the patriarchal image of an almighty invincible father god needs to be challenged and reconstructed.[20]

6. *Create new rituals.* Rituals help challenge the old and establish the new. To make them more palatable, use old, familiar steps to ease into the new celebrations — which is just what conference leaders did on the last day, during Sunday morning's alternative to a traditional church service. The "blessing of milk and honey" ritual simply followed the format of a traditional communion service.

The women sang, but not about Jesus. They celebrated

with two elements, but not bread and wine. They mentioned God and grace, but the new meanings reflected the pagan context. They celebrated freedom, but mocked the only One who could set them free.

Clinking their glasses of rice milk, they shared in a dramatic responsive reading and singing rite. The speakers read — with drama and feeling — the lines of the prayer below (the most erotic suggestions were banished to the endnotes). "Sophia Creator God . . ." sang the exuberant women between each part. "Let your milk and honey flow . . . Sophia . . . Sophia. . . ." Over and over and over. . . .

> Our maker Sophia, we are women in your image. With the hot blood of our wombs we give form to new life. . . .
> *[All:] Sophia, Creator God, let your milk and honey flow. . . . Shower us with your love. . . .*
> Our mother Sophia, we are women in your image. With the milk of our breasts we suckle the children. . . .
> *Sophia, Creator God. . . .*
> Our guide Sophia, we are women in your image. With our moist mouths we kiss away a tear. . . . With the honey of wisdom in our mouths we prophesy a full humanity to all peoples.
> *Sophia, Creator God. . . .*
> (All drink of the milk and honey.)
> Sophia, we celebrate your life-giving energy which pulses through our veins. . . .
> *Halleluya! Pelo tsa rona. . . .*[21]
> We celebrate our unique perspectives, intelligence . . . our guides, our spiritual mothers, our models.
> *Halleluya! Pelo tsa rona. . . .*
> We celebrate the nourishment of your milk and honey. Through the sharing of this holy

manna [could be a hidden reference to "Mana:" Moon Mother, creative energy, Goddess of Creation and death] we enter into community which strengthens and renews us for the struggle.

Halleluya! Pelo tsa rona. . . .

We celebrate sensual life you give us. . . . We celebrate the fingertips vibrating upon the skin of a love. We celebrate the tongue which licks a wound or wets our lips. We celebrate our bodiliness, our physicality, the sensations of pleasure, our oneness with earth and water.[22]

"Not surprisingly, Sophia seemed to reserve a special blessing for lesbian love," observed Kathy Kersten. "The prayer above was read by individual women, except for the 'vibrating fingertips' line, which was read by two women together."[23]

The more sensual and shocking expressions help speed the planned paradigm shift. They cause what educators call cognitive dissonance — a form of mental confusion that forces people to rethink and stretch their old values to accommodate new ideas and experiences. Their end justifies the means, argue the radical feminists, and their planned end is total cultural transformation. If they have their way, every family, community, business, and church would have to conform to feminist beliefs and values. (If you question this statement, don't wait — read chapter 9 now.)

Feminism Everywhere

If feminist activists only eyed the church, they wouldn't make such an impact. But their vision aims far beyond spiritual issues, and our social climate supports their agenda. Their sisterhood stretches around the world, and their voices ring out from every corner of our culture: Hollywood, the media, schools, publishing houses. . . . Some of the links may never connect with each other. Yet, as if pulled by an invisible puppet master, they share one message: Social and spiritual revolution now! Death to male leadership in politics, economics, entertainment, churches, and — don't forget — heaven! Equality within the present culture is not enough! Long live feminist socialism, feminist politics, and feminist spirituality.

Each small victory strengthens the whole movement. The further the message spreads, the faster the transformation. In the end, everything that agrees with feminist visions must be seen as good and right. Everything that conflicts with their vision must be considered bad — harmful to the "common good," the envisioned collective society.

Box office sensations such as *Pocahontas* speed the process. Illustrating Disney's "new genre" of politically correct movies, it gave us an enticing look at the world from a pantheistic perspective. Since its heroine models the feminist ideal — and since its videos and books perpetuate its neo-pagan suggestions, let's take a look at the way it changes popular consciousness.

You remember the popular Disney story, don't you? Brave, assertive, and free-spirited, the Indian maiden scales mountains, climbs trees, and steers a canoe better than a man. Like "Women Who Run with Wolves,"[24] she does what she wants — and submits to no one.

"What is my path?" she asks the wise old spirit of Grandmother Willow, a magical tree in the forest. "How am I ever going to find it?"

"Listen," says her enchanted counselor. "All around you are spirits, child. They live in the earth, the water, the sky. If you listen, they will guide you."

Like the women at the Re-imagining Conference, the Indian maiden believes. Why shouldn't she? Not only does the tree spirit's advice fit the context of Disney's fictionalized history, it also fits the human inclination to trust earthy spirits and mystical forces. Few mothers realize that when they and their children see the world from a pantheistic perspective, even Christian words take on new meanings.

The Disney story points an angry finger at the world's new villain: the white males who have come to exploit the land and steal its gold. Even handsome John Smith is made to look foolish compared to the nature-wise woman he loves. Their exchange of wisdom flows one way only: from Indian to European. So when Smith unwittingly offers to build English cities on Indian lands, Pocahontas shows her disgust, then sings him a lesson on pagan oneness: everything is filled with spiritual life and linked in a never-ending circle.

It all makes sense when you watch the movie. With subtle mastery, its makers highlight the anti-Western message and stir predictable indignation: How can the crude British sailors, so ignorant of spiritual things, call natives "heathen"? Those arrogant intruders are the real savages who batter the earth and rob its friends.

In contrast, the natives seem flawless. They care for the land. They commune with its spirits. They love each other and enjoy their children. Kekata, the tribal shaman or medicine man, provides spiritual protection and guidance. The ghostly images in the smoke from his magic fire warn the tribe to shun the newcomers who "prowl the earth like ravenous wolves." The only exception is John Smith, who has learned to see life and nature from Pocahontas' perspective. Awakened to the peaceful ways of pantheism, he risks his life to stop the war.

The deep spiritual insights come from women. As feminist and multicultural lessons tell us: patriarchy brings war and oppression; matriarchy brings love and wisdom — especially if the female heroines are non-Western. It doesn't matter if the source of matriarchal wisdom comes from humans, ancestral spirits, or nature spirits. So when chief Powhatan feels the spirit of Pocahontas' dead mother guiding him, he heeds her lofty wisdom: "There will be no more killing. Let us be guided instead to a place of peace."

What About the Facts?

The true story about Pocahontas would have undermined Disney's politically correct message. It tells about a girl between 10 and 14 years old, who saved John Smith's life, and helped the settlers of the Jamestown colony. They, in turn, shared their Christian faith with her. Pocahontas apparently accepted Christ and was baptized. After she married John Rolfe, the two traveled to England where she was "received at the court."[25] Before her return to her native land, the brave 22 year old died of smallpox.

Pocahontas' tribe belonged to the Algonquin family, a nation at war long before European settlers came. Dr. Clark Wissler, an anthropologist recognized as a world authority on the American Indian, tells how the "warlike" Iroquois invaded Algonquin country.

Like other nations throughout history — Babylonians, Greek, Aztec, English, etc.—they expanded into new territories. "The Algonquin were not merely at war with Iroquois but often with each other. There were about a hundred Algonquin tribes. . . . In revenge for past injuries, a few members of one tribe would stealthily approach the camp of a hostile tribe, take a scalp or two and escape. . . . The highest honors went to the man who was the most daring and ruthless in such raids."[26]

But, you may argue, that was written by a male tainted by the bias of Western racism. Actually, Dr. Wissler's research shows deep respect for American Indians. What he wrote about their violence was just as true of other earth-centered nations around the world.

Brutality has always characterized cultures inspired by human nature and empowered by occult forces. Some of the worst stories came from my native Norway and describe the ancient pre-Christian Vikings. While the cruelties of ancient Babylonian, Egyptian, and Aztec civilizations are well documented, we need look no further back than to Bosnia and Rwanda in the 1990s to see barbarian expressions of human cruelty.

Disney simply twisted the facts. Remember, history documents Pocahontas' conversion to Christianity, not Smith's conversion to pantheism.

But do the facts really matter? After all, this is only a Disney movie!

While they may not matter to those who sell entertainment, they should matter to leaders who are looking for models on which to base a new civilization. But they don't, and columnist Thomas Sowell, Senior Fellow at the Hoover Institution at Stanford University, is concerned. In his article, "The Right to Infiltrate," he warns us that the "leftist intelligentsia," which includes leading feminists, "know they are in a cultural war, as those on the other side often do not." What's worse, *Only one side is battling. That is why they are winning.*[27] Sowell then shows us another reason:

> Was the feminist movement discredited when its claim that Superbowl Sunday was the day when the most wives were battered could not be supported by any evidence? Has Paul Ehrlich or the Worldwatch Institute been discredited by the repeated failures of their hysterical [environmental] predictions? . . .
>
> *Being factual does not matter to those who are politically correct.* Some of the bolder members of the anointed have openly expressed the view that various racial charges which turned out to be *hoaxes do not bother them because these charges serve to raise consciousness.* Similarly, some of the brassier feminists declare that they are untroubled by false charges against some men because men in general are guilty of the things charged.[28]

Sowell is suggesting that today's cultural battle will be

won in the arena of consciousness, where propaganda means more than facts, and feminist anger wields more influence than science. If he is right, what will happen to Christian values? Who will be the new common enemy? Which paradigm will define our words and steer the new world?

Disney's massive media empire represents the kind of capitalism and male power that spiritual feminists love to hate. Yet, the two opposites share a common goal: to shift America's consciousness from a Judeo/Christian world view into the New Age/feminist paradigm.[29] It's easy. Like today's advertisers who pay millions for televised mini-exposures, they know that facts and logic matter little. What counts are messages that *seem* right and *feel* good.

THE BASIS FOR SOCIAL CONSCIOUSNESS . . .	
Old Paradigm	**New Paradigm**
Truth	Social and pagan myths
Facts	Feelings and experience
Observation	Imagination
Logic	Speculation
Science	Politicized pseudo-science
Reality	Fantasy
Factual history	Storytelling

The old-paradigm ways of communicating fit neither the new paradigm nor the feminist kingdom. Kingdom, of course, is a misnomer. The feminist vision knows neither king nor boundaries. Since it sees the world through the new-paradigm lens, it can only appreciate feminist ideals. It demands tolerance and respect for whatever it deems "good" and shows no tolerance for those who disagree.

The shift from facts to feelings protects religious feminists against contrary evidence. The historical record doesn't shake their convictions, for their guides have re-imagined history. Scientific evidence doesn't ruffle their faith, for the new paradigm "transcends science." Logic doesn't matter, for it has been dismissed as an obsolete tool of patriarchy.

Ponder the implications for a moment. What would happen to justice if, as in former times, it is subject to the whims of superstition, angry crowds, and pagan curses? Chapters 6 and 8 will give some answers. Meanwhile, enjoy the good news.

The Kingdom of God

The rest of this book will leave little doubt that America is drifting back into the shadows of paganism. The key question is not how to stop the spreading darkness. It is how we can bring the light of hope into the world's dark and confusing places. How, as ambassadors of God's kingdom, can we bring His love to those who are stumbling their way through the confusing pathways of the new spirituality.

But first, take a look at His kingdom. Compare it with the world that feminists envision.

1. *God's kingdom is eternal.* It has always existed and will never end.

The feminists can make no such claim for their envisioned reign. From their evolutionary perspective, everything always changes. They can hope for something better but they can never be sure, for their goddess is a capricious ruler.

2. *It is other-worldly.* In stark contrast to the feminist this-world utopia, Jesus says, "My kingdom is not of this world."[30] Those who love Him understand this, for neither are they. The world has rarely appreciated God's true friends, for their beliefs made no sense to those who prefer the opposite paradigm. "The world has hated them," said Jesus, "for they are not of the world any more than I am of the world."[31]

3. *It cannot be understood through human wisdom.* Inner wisdom sounds good to women who idolize self, but

it blinds them to the knowledge of God. Only those who walk by His light can comprehend His wonders.

"It has been given to you to know the mysteries of the kingdom of heaven, but to them it has not been given," said Jesus to His friends. "I speak to them in parables, because seeing they do not see, and hearing they do not hear, nor do they understand" (Matt. 13:11–13).

4. *It is holy.* The "sacred spaces" of Sophia devotees are not. Feminist attempts to re-imagine their world only makes it more unholy. No one can blend the two kingdoms. For "what fellowship can light have with darkness? What agreement is there between the temple of God and idols? For we are the temple of the living God. As God has said: 'I will live with them and walk among them, and I will be their God, and they will be my people.' Therefore come out from them and be separate" (2 Cor. 6:14–17).

5. *It has only one door: Jesus Christ.* This truth infuriates those who envision a global spirituality that will unite all the religions of the world. Clinging to pagan illusions, they spurn God's offer to make them holy. All other religions demand human work for spiritual salvation. Only Christ invites everyone to the Cross and to His kingdom — no matter how low they have fallen. But that sounds absurd to Sophia's devotees. "For the message of the cross is foolishness to those who are perishing, but to us who are being saved it is the power of God" (1 Cor. 1:18).

6. *One can only enter as a child.*[32] The key is child-likeness, not child-ishness. Gibberish and mindlessness are childish. Trust and humility are child-like. Free from an accumulated baggage of anger, bitterness, and emotional defenses, children simply hear and believe.

7. *It will make up for all the world's pain and injustice.* One day, God will settle the score for all the hurts and cruelties suffered in a world ruled by human whims and ambitions. He never promised freedom from suffering and abuse in this life. To the contrary, he foretold both His own

crucifixion and the persecution His friends would endure for their faith. "I have told you these things," He said, "so that in me you may have peace. In this world you will have trouble. But take heart! I have overcome the world" (John 16:33).

The next chapter will show what happens when people try to manipulate occult forces with the human will. The process is as old as time — and no less dangerous to genuine peace than it was when humans first sought to be like God.

Endnotes

[1]Naomi R. Goldenberg, *Changing of the Gods: Feminism & the End of Traditional Religions* (Boston, MA: Beacon Press, 1979), p. 3.

[2]Alla Bozarth-Campbell, *Womanpriest: A Personal Odyssey* (North Carolina State Press, 1978), back cover.

[3]Marianne Williamson, *A Woman's Worth* (New York, NY: Ballantine Books, 1993), p. 10.

[4]Luke 24:45. See also Luke 10:21; Matthew 13:16; Ephesians 1:18.

[5]Isaiah 43:4.

[6]Read *Evidence that Demands a Verdict* and *More Evidence that Demands a Verdict* by Josh McDowell (Nashville, TN: Thomas Nelson Publishers, 1992).

[7]Kathleen Fischer, *Women at the Well* (New York, NY: Paulist Press, 1988), p. 6. The words deleted in the first sentence were: "to any spiritual direction context."

[8]Re-Imagining Conference, tape 1-1, side B.

[9]Ibid.

[10]Goldenberg, *Changing of the Gods*, p. 3.

[11]Ibid.

[12]Fischer, *Women at the Well*, p. 5, 6, 7, 10, 12.

[13]Re-Imagining Conference, tape 3-2, side A. Kwok Pui-Lan is identified in the program booklet as a graduate of Harvard Divinity School and is now an associate professor of theology at the Episcopal Divinity School in Cambridge, Massachusetts.

[14]Isaiah 6:8–10.

[15]Re-Imagining Conference, tape 2-2, side A.

[16]Re-Imagining Conference, tape 4-1, side B and tape 4-2, side A.

[17]Re-Imagining Conference, tape 4-2, side A. Elizabeth Bettenhausen is coordinator of the Study/Action Program at the Women's Theological Center in Boston, Massachusetts.

[18]Psalm 119:105.

[19]Re-Imagining Conference, tape 9-1, side A.

[20]Re-Imagining Conference, tape 10-1, side A.

[21]Halleluya! We sing your praises. . . . The important question to ask is: whose praises? The god or goddess worshipped at this ritual was not the biblical God.

[22]Re-Imagining Conference, tape 12-1, side B. These lines were part of the prayer to Sophia: "With our warm body fluids we remind the world of its pleasures and sensations. . . . Our sweet Sophia, With [deleted words] we invite a lover, we birth a child"

[23]Kathy Kersten, "God in Your Mirror?" *Lutheran Commentator* (May/ June 1994), p. 7.

[24]*Women Who Run With Wolves,* the title of a top-selling book by Clarissa Pinkola Estes, who gives many names to woman who has unleashed her wildness and lives with abandon: The Light from the Abyss, the Wolverine, the Spider Woman, the Wolf Woman, Death Goddess, and Woman Who Lives at the Edge of the World. Cited by Clark Morphew, "Religion and Ethics," Saint Paul Pioneer Press, October 29, 1994.

[25]*Encyclopedia Britannica*, Vol. 18 (Chicago, IL: William Benton, 1968), p. 85.

[26]Clark Wissler, *Indians of the United States* (New York, NY: Anchor Book, 1940), p. 70-71.

[27]Thomas Sowell, "The Right to Infiltrate," *Forbes* (March 13, 1995); p. 74.

[28]Ibid.

[29]Tim Wildmon, "Why American Families Should Boycott Disney," American Family Association, Tupelo, Mississippi.

[30]John 18:36.

[31]John 17:14.

[32]Matthew 18:2.

Chapter 4

Your Will Be Done,

or

My Will Be Done?

෴

Thousands of us have come to Earth at this time with the single wild determination to create a new world. . . . We are trying to remember how to be goddesses.[1] (Sonia Johnson, author of *Wild-fire: Igniting the She/Volution*)

In Witchcraft, we do not fight self-interest; we follow it.[2] (Starhawk)

If anyone wants to do His will, he shall know. (John 7:17)

෴

On a misty autumn morning, I drove across the San Fransciso Bay Bridge toward Berkeley, home of the University of California, the Free Speech movement, and a host of other spirited causes. Scanning the gray, watery expanse beyond the guardrails, I prayed, "Lord, help me really listen to Tracy. Give her freedom to share her heart with me. Please show her Your love through me — and prepare her to hear You."

I knew Tracy through an environmental group in Kansas City. At the time, I was writing a book showing how neo-paganism permeates the environmental movement and hides God's concern for His creation. Each time I called Tracy, she was more than willing to answer all my questions. So when she planned a visit to the Bay Area to visit a local seminary, she called me to see if we could get together.

"Sure," I told her. "I'll be your tour guide for a day. Where would you like to go? To the ocean? To a redwood forest. . . ?"

She was quick to answer. "Muir Woods."

A few weeks later I picked her up in Berkeley, and as we drove together toward the forested foothills of Mount Tamalpais near the ocean, God began to answer my prayer. Before we even reached the redwood forest, she had told me that she was a witch, a lesbian, and an elementary school teacher.

With her short brown hair and friendly smile, Tracy looked more like a college student than a witch. Yet her blend of pagan spirituality, sensuality, and evangelistic zeal didn't surprise me. As you saw earlier, an inordinate number of neo-pagans have chosen professions like teaching which provide effective platforms for transforming our culture. Like the rest of us, they want to build a kinder world — one that reflects their love for nature and quest for "good, not evil" power.

We found the forest, parked the car, and walked a short distance to the first cluster of towering trees. In silence, we gazed up at the canopy of lacy green branches and breathed the unforgettable fragrance of redwood, ferns, and forest floor. For a moment the shared joy in the presence of one of God's masterpieces broke through all our human and spiritual differences. Slowly we started up a trail winding between the massive red trunks and the soft green ferns.

"If you love nature so much, how can you be a Christian?" asked Tracy after a while.

"Why does that surprise you?" I asked.

"Your God separated people from the earth. We believe in oneness with nature."

I prayed for words that would speak to her heart. "Tracy, I don't see a contradiction," I began. "I believe in oneness with the God who created all this beauty. He loves it, and He fills me with the same kind of love."

"But Christians don't take care of it." Her statement seemed more like a question than an accusation.

"You mean Christians here in America this last century?"

"And in Europe. Look at all the polluted rivers and oceans. . . ."

"That's happening all over the world. Wherever there's a lot of people, there's pollution. But, hasn't America done more to clean up its air and rivers than most pantheistic or polytheistic cultures?"[3]

She thought for a moment. "But pagans care more about nature. Christians are too materialistic. They use more of earth's resources."

"I'm not sure that genuine Christians do. A lot of people call themselves Christian just because they grew up in western culture. They live just like the rest of the world, buying what they want because it's there. Christians who are one with Jesus Christ are probably not caught up in materialism. They want to follow Jesus, who was willing to give up everything in order to show us His way."[4]

We walked on, quieted by the fragrance and majesty of the towering trees. Silently we listened to the whispers of the wind in the treetops. They reminded me of the kindness of my Creator and I felt a surge of joy.

"Tracy, I pray when I sense God's presence," I said. "Do you pray to the goddess?"

"No," she answered, "we don't pray. We call it 'doing magic.' "

I pondered her words. "Doing magic." The opposite of

prayer. Women who "do magic" command spiritual forces to fulfill their human will. Prayer means aligning our will to God's will and asking Him to intercede.[5] His will versus her will! Struck by the immensity of the spiritual chasm between us, I glanced at Tracy. We both wanted to do what was right and good, but her good was the opposite of mine.

As we walked and talked, I learned more about her Wiccan ways, and Tracy began to see a whole new side of Christianity. When I finally left her in Berkeley at the end of the day, she suggested we meet again.

I haven't heard from Tracy since then. Perhaps her spiritual journey drove her too far into the embrace of occult powers to risk another Christian encounter — and the spiritual confusion that often follows. Women who have just tasted the initial delights of occult empowerment are seldom ready to give them up. They may try different paths, but their feelings suggest that paganism is right. Few will heed contrary evidence until the sweetness turns bitter. Even then, it's not easy to give up the intoxicating vision of supernatural power to do "my will, my way."

Empowering *My* Will

In April 1995 a friend sent me a registration form for a day-long women's conference called "Releasing the Spirit: Women at Play." She had found it at her local library.

"I think it's inter-denominational, not just Catholic," she said. "Does it fit your research?"

"I think it does," I said, thanking her.

Two months later, I drove into the Archbishop Mitty High School in San Jose, California. At the parking lot entrance stood three persons holding signs. I had time to read the first one. "Catholic Women's Network is anti-Catholic, feminist, New Age, anti-male priest," it said.

Everyone seemed to be entering through the cafeteria, where groups of women were drinking coffee, talking, and checking the resource displays. I passed by the crowds surrounding the four book tables, scanned the craft displays and freebie tables, headed for the last large group of tables, and squeezed into a small opening between the browsers and shoppers. From a rack in front of me dangled dozens of silvery rectangles with engraved geometric signs. I lifted one and read the description.

"Odin, the 13th Rune, symbol of death and rebirth."

A Rune! An old Norwegian form of divination. I should have known, but the ones I saw in Norway long ago were cut in stone, not on metal, and were not used as necklaces.

Another rack held ornaments with more familiar symbols: the Egyptian ankh, the yin yang, and lots of goblins and crosses. I lifted a large flat cross. Six other symbols were stamped into its surface. Its center showed a quartered circle, the familiar power sign of contemporary Wiccans (witches). Native Americans call it the medicine wheel. The four arms of the cross sported a pentagram, a hexagram, the yin yang, and the Hindu ohm. This event was turning out to be more pagan than I had expected.

The last rack hid an assortment of tools for women's rituals: incense, candles, rattles, and drums. One drum was decorated with a triquetra, an ancient symbol of the female trinity made popular by modern followers of the goddess. It reminded me of a statement by the Wiccan leader Starhawk. "To cast a spell is to project energy through a symbol," she wrote in *The Spiral Dance,* her popular manual for witchcraft.[6] Apparently, any pagan symbol can be used to channel power at will, but the drum is the favorite tool for invoking spirits at the start of a ritual.

I noticed a sage wand that looked just like the one used in the Sophia Circle I had visited earlier. "This gift from ME/ Father Spirit has been crafted in Sedona," explained the label. "We invite you to use this magical smoke to cleanse, bless yourselves and your surroundings, and to create an atmosphere of peace and healing."

What a lie! I recognized the two letters "ME." They have become a popular symbol for a new unholy union: Mother Earth and Me. Universal energy and my will. Like a secret message for the initiated, this formula crops up in Girl Scout literature, environmental curriculum, books, cartoons, etc.

Next to the drums were small bags labeled "Casting with Runes." I picked one up. It felt heavy. Inside were the same silvery runes I saw earlier. A small booklet told their history: "Runes were used by the shamans and healers of Scandinavia to heal their sick and cast spells. . . . " In other words, to empower people to do their will.

I turned to the next tiny page. "Smudge yourself and your runes with sage or incense to cleanse and purify the energy," it said, sounding more Native American and Buddhist than Norwegian. "Sit quietly, hold the rune in your hand, take three deep breaths. . . ."

"Can I show you how to use them?" asked a young woman dressed in a white flowing gown.

"Please do," I answered, handing her the bag while repeating Psalm 18 in my mind.

"They were used by the Vikings to find direction. We use them to see ourselves and find our path," she said, blending an historical fact with modern selfism.

She turned away for a moment to answer someone. When she returned, I was ready with another question. "That's an interesting dress you're wearing," I said. "Does it have a special meaning?"

"It's a ritual attire."

"Ritual attire?"

"Yes. Sort of a goddess gown." She spun around, and the light, loose fabric flowed softly after her.

"Any particular goddess?"

"For me it's Aphrodite, but you can be anything you want to be. The goddess is a lady of a thousand names. When you put it on, you feel different. Sort of special. Like wearing a mask for Halloween."

"Where did you find this gown?"

The kits are over there." She pointed to a distant corner. "They're separate pieces. With these special fasteners — she pointed to the clips at each shoulder, you can put them together any way you want to."

"What about your hat?" I glanced at her three-sided velvet headdress.

"It means anything you want it to mean. Any goddess you want to be."

She seemed so proud of her pagan outfit — and so oblivious to the dangers of the religion she so heartily embraced. Blue-eyed and red-haired, she looked young and innocent. How many of her peers were following the same path?

"How did you learn about all this?" I asked.

"I read a lot."

I wanted to ask more questions, but by now the cafeteria was almost empty. So I thanked her, grabbed a cup of coffee, and hurried after the rest.

The program guide showed an opening ritual — perhaps "casting a sacred circle." I didn't want to participate, but neither did I want to expose my beliefs and shut out personal encounters this early in the day. "Please show me what to do next, Lord," I prayed as I hurried to the gym.

A woman stopped me at the entrance. "I'm sorry, but you can't bring coffee in here," she said.

"Thank you. I'll just wait out here," I said, and stepped back. Behind me was the open doorway of an unlit room. "Thank you, Lord," I whispered as I backed unnoticed into the little sanctuary and sat down on the only chair inside the tiny office — His special refuge for me. Hidden from sight, I watched the ceremony.

The Sacred Circle

"We welcome your energies and spirits," began the president of the Catholic Women's Network. "There are almost 500 women here. . . . Some of you have come a long way — you're from Pennsylvania, Iowa, Chicago, Texas, Oregon, Colorado . . . and 77 cities in California."

A strange deep sound began to reverberate through the room. Someone was blowing into a conch shell and the sound rose like a mystical trumpet call. Then the ritual began. About 200 women formed an inner circle. The rest formed a large outer circle. All joined hands and echoed the words of a simple chant:

> Make a circle, make a circle, call it sacred place. . . .

"Holy is Your name," I prayed silently from my little sanctuary.

"Make a circle, call it sacred place," intoned five hundred voices.

The leader spoke and the women echoed her words: "North and East and South meets West and night is chased by day."

"Make a circle, make a circle . . ." chanted the swaying group. "We are summoned by our dark to chase our fears away."

Summoned by our dark? The words startled me. What did they mean? In pagan cultures, people invoke certain spirits to protect them against more obviously evil spirits. Was there any connection? Or was it more of a Jungian belief about the dark side of self?

"We are summoned by the light to work and love and play."

"Make a circle, call it sacred place. . . ."

The repetitions seemed endless — almost unbearable. After a while, I covered my ears, hoping to escape the pagan words and hypnotic rhythm. The circle of moving bodies swayed and flowed, on and on. . . .

When the chant finally ended, the prayers began — to the four directions, the spirits, the goddess, to whomever.

"Pray for the things that we want!" instructed the leader.

"We want some energy!" shouted someone.

"We want some joy!"

"We want to feel okay!"

"We want our sexuality!"

"We want to be released . . . free!"

"Oh God," I whispered, "You offered us all this, but we've turned our back to You. I am so sorry."

Someone was reciting a new version of Proverbs 8, the favorite Scripture to those who seek a feminine God. "There I was beside Him," she said, "God's delight . . . at play day by day. I found delight in everything. . . . Little did I know. . . ." At this point the familiar Scripture evolved into a gross distortion of truth and a bitter personal testimony of burnout, depression, hospitalization. "I had to turn in Jesus . . . I had to get a better deal."

What did she find in His place? It wasn't clear. She ended with a pretense of laughter. "Ha-Ha, ho-ho!" she laughed stiffly and loudly. "Just practice it. Ha-ha, ho-ho!"

It made no sense, but everybody did what they were told. "Ha-ha, ho-ho! Ha-ha. . . ."

A woman shared her testimony in dance and words. She told of childhood abuse, visions of God, disillusionment, and despair. She gave no answers, only the acknowledgment that women suffer, are angry, want solutions. Like seekers at the Renaissance of the Sacred Feminine Conference, the women were prompted to search for real or imagined pain in themselves. Was this the "spiritual nourishment" the conference brochures had promised us? It seemed so futile.

Another chant began:

God-me, me-god, play play play-ing. God-me, me-God. . . .

Women as God, God as woman — the essence of

feminist sacredness! Amazing! How could we willingly trade the power of the sovereign King of the universe for hollow affirmations and hopeless testimonies? Is this really what women want?

The meeting ended with a loud expression of feminist assertiveness — one I had heard in the Sophia Circle: "Ye-ah, ye-ah, ye-ah." Then we all left for our first workshop.

My Word, My Will

From a list of 28 workshops, I could only pick two. I quickly eliminated options such as Mantras and Chants, 3D Mandalas, Sacred Play, Laugh Way to Happiness, and Drum Fun. I had seen more than enough ritual tools for manipulating power, and the morning's "play" time was more crude than funny. I chose a workshop titled "Feminism and Christianity in Conversation." It met in the chapel.

"What we see is the move of the spirit around the world," began the leader, Dr. Regina Coll, an international lecturer and director of field education at the University of Notre Dame. "The old image . . . is that God was the judge waiting for us to make an error so He can get us. . . . What is developing now is a metaphor for God. . . . The mother image must be developed. . . ."

Many women have been wounded by legalistic churches.[7] Dr. Coll had illustrated a genuine problem, but her answer would conceal the only lasting solution. Like the leaders of the Re-imagining Conference, she challenged her class to create new images of God — images that would free a woman to do her own will without any shame. "Think what your gut, not head, reaction is when I say God is a mother . . . God is a judge . . . a lover . . . a child."

The responses came in rapid succession:

"Mother reminds me of grace."

"When I think of God as lover, I think of bodily eroticism."

"Feminist images 'seem to be more playful.' "

Yes, like the mythical goddesses they imitate, I thought.

"God is more me than I am myself. Are we convinced of that?" continued Dr. Coll. "God-me, me-God. Someone said, 'I found god in myself and I loved her fiercely.' "

Someone at the Re-imagining Conference had used the same quote.[8] Some phrases are repeated so often they become part of our mind-set and the cultural consciousness.

Having changed the image of God into an imitation of a permissive and lovable self, Coll took time to re-define some traditional words that might quench self-expression or produce old-fashioned guilt. Ponder these new definitions that flowed between teacher and learners:

* Pride: Women don't have enough pride. We forget the second commandment: love yourself.
* Sin: It's not loving ourselves enough.
* The Cross: We need resurrection, not crucifixion.
* Virgin: She who is complete in herself. Her identity is not dependent on others.

No one questioned this freedom to change the Bible. Perhaps no one knew what it really said.[9] Maybe the euphoria of defying the King of the universe quenched all caution. The women obviously enjoyed tearing down the barriers to doing their will. To clear up the distortions, look how God uses the same words in the New Testament:

* Pride: The attitude that we are good enough on our own and don't need God, or claiming personal credit for something God, not we, accomplished.
* Sin: Missing the mark. Falling short of God's standard for rightness.
* The Cross: God's solution for our sin. There can be no resurrection without the Cross. "I have been crucified with Christ; it is no longer I who live, but Christ lives in me" (Gal. 2:20).
* Virgin: A woman who has never had sexual intercourse.

Sobered by the disdain for God's Word, I joined the lunch line and looked around. How many of these 500 women shared the blind delight of challenging God's authority? What could I say that might open their eyes? I didn't know.

Turkey or vegetarian? Awakened to the choice of the moment, I chose the turkey sandwich and joined three other women at a table on the patio. We were all from different church backgrounds — Lutheran, Baptist, Episcopalian, and Catholic. Two women had found what they wanted — non-traditional churches with feel-good messages, fun celebrations, and "respect" for all genders.

The afternoon skits in the gym helped stretch our moral boundaries. Having re-defined our Maker, the women could now re-design their bodies. A sensual dancer demonstrated every body pad and slimming device available. Strange, since they are also taught to deny sexual differences.

"Jesus, I am so sorry," joked the dancer. "I didn't intend to include words like ecstasy and passion." Everyone laughed.

The afternoon workshop taught another lesson in revising truth to speak our will. "We are the authoritarian authors of the Bible — we can decide what this means," said Margie, our leader. "The varnish on its pages is what [traditional church] people say it means. Sandpaper the varnish, and there'll be nothing left."

Determined to turn her students into varnish-removers, she pretended to read her Bible with its old varnish still intact. "I should read the Bible," she mocked, opened it to Genesis, and started to snore.

She turned to the New Testament and read a familiar story. "Jesus is asleep. . . . The storm frightens the disciples. They wake him. . . . He says, 'Peace, be still.' " She looked at us questioningly.

"Wrong varnish!" she laughed. "She yells at the storm."

Adding her own varnish to another passage, she told us

Jesus was snarling at a woman who asked for help. How did she come to that conclusion? I raised my hand three times to ask. Three times she glanced away as if she didn't notice. Perhaps she suspected that I might ask contrary questions.

From Defiance to Witchcraft

Mockery is one of the essential steps in the paradigm shift. It always has been part of cultural transformation. Remember, back in the garden of Eden, Eve was content with all God's beautiful gifts until the serpent focused her mind on the forbidden fruit. Even when her desire was awakened, she would have resisted the temptation had the serpent not raised doubts about God's instructions. Notice the tone of his question: "Has God indeed said . . . ?"

Eve knew the consequences of eating the fruit, but the deceiver put a new spin on the truth she had learned — turning it into a subtle yet monstrous lie:

> You will not surely die. For God knows that in the day you eat of it your eyes will be opened, and you will be like God, knowing good and evil." So when the woman saw that the tree was good for food, that it was pleasant to the eyes, and a tree desirable to make one wise, she took of its fruit and ate. She also gave to her husband with her, and he ate. Then the eyes of both of them were opened, and they knew that they were naked (Gen. 3:1–7).

They had lost their innocence, and they knew it. Aware that God had seen their sin, they hid. No longer free to face reality or feel good about themselves, they rationalized their actions and blamed each other. In the end, following feelings rather than truth brought alienation, not happiness.

Feminists put their own spin on that first deception: "Even if God did say you couldn't, so what? Eve was the true heroine. She models the boldness needed to destroy patriarchy. It's time we write our own Bible."

When feminist leaders began to write their own gospel (we'll look at it in chapter 7), they soon discovered a missing ingredient: spiritual power. Accomplishing their will required a new power source. Like humanist leaders who eventually embraced cosmic spirituality, secular feminists turned to ancient myths and pagan formulas.

The following chart is adapted from my book *Brave New Schools*. Notice that humanism was only a step on the way from Christianity to paganism.

CHRISTIANITY	HUMANISM	RELIGIOUS
(Biblical Absolutes) Old Religion	(Relative Values) Killed Religion	(Global Absolutes) Establishes "New" Religion
The Bible reveals reality	Science explains reality	Feelings and experience define reality
God is transcendent and personal	God is a non-existent crutch	A pantheistic god(dess) or force is present in all
Trusting God is key to success	Trusting self is key to success	Trusting one's inner god-self is key to success
Good and evil are incompatible	Good and evil are relative	Joining good and evil brings wholeness

In *The Spiral Dance*, a much-quoted manual on contemporary witchcraft, Starhawk shows what it takes to manipulate occult forces. Please don't think this is too irrelevant and then close the book. Many of her suggestions are now seeping into church rituals or "celebrations." For instance, the Re-Imagining leaders prepared a sacred space at the beginning of the conference. Look why this is important.

"Each ritual," explains the founder of the Covenant of the Goddess, "begins with the creation of a sacred space, the 'casting of a circle,' which establishes a temple. Goddess and God are then invoked or awakened within each participant and are considered to be personally present within the circle and the bodies of the worshippers. Power is raised through chanting or dancing and may be directed through a symbol or visualization."[10]

While rituals may involve a group, each pagan is her own master. She submits to no one. When Starhawk was first challenged by a spirit (or demon) to pursue "Witchy work," she answered, "I'll go, but only on my own terms."[11] Having entered a trance, she "saw" a host of spirits join the first one and shout in unison, "How could you ever do anything on any other terms but your own?"

"Witchy work" is mainly magic — and, according to Starhawk, it's easy. All it takes to begin is "four basic abilities: relaxation, concentration, visualization, and projection."[12] Do they sound familiar? They become a major doorway to demonic realms when used together to alter one's consciousness. The final — and culturally acceptable — step is to project energy by moving one's mental images with the imagination. That's the essence of magic and spells.[13]

Starhawk spreads the lures of feminist empowerment to Christian groups and seminaries as well as covens.[14] As a witch, she teaches the timeless rituals of earth-centered spirituality. Yet her power is no different than the impersonal Hindu "prana" power taught at the Re-imagining Conference. In fact, Starhawk's words seem to echo those of the Korean theologian Chung Hyun Kyung. "Relax and feel yourself rooted in the earth," she tells a counselee. "Feel the energy enter . . . move up through your body . . . up past your head, your Third Eye . . . out the top of your head."[15]

New Names for Old Rites

Church counselors who use similar formulas for healing may call this energy "the Holy Spirit" or "Jesus." Christian labels make these rituals acceptable. Once they are introduced to a church, few realize that they match Starhawk's seven steps up the spine to the Third Eye as well as what Hindu and Buddhist teachers call kundalini — the feminine force of tantric yoga.

A desperate father called me one day to find help for his adult daughter who was tormented by what he called "the kundalini."

"What do you think the kundalini is?" I asked.

"It is a force in everybody. Everybody has it."

"Who told you that?"

"Her therapist. She regressed her to her past lives."

"Are you a Christian?"

"Of course!" He sounded insulted.

"Is your daughter a Christian?"

"Yes, of course she is."

"Do you think your therapist is a Christian?"

"They all were."

I suggested that no genuine Christian therapist or counselor would use hypnotic regression therapy nor validate belief in reincarnation or past lives. He sounded surprised, so I quoted Hebrews 9:27: "It is appointed for men to die once, but after this the judgment."

He listened as I explained that kundalini came from Hindu or Buddhist forms of tantric yoga. If his daughter indeed had a tormenting spirit inside her, whether her counselors call it kundalini or any other name, it would be demonic. She might need deliverance, I told him, and suggested someone who could help her start a relationship with Jesus Christ that could keep her free from tormenting spirits.

The original kundalini yoga rituals shed their harsh disciplines years ago, when they were introduced to Western seekers. Americans preferred tamer versions of tantric yoga, the kinds they could adapt to their own spiritual and sexual lifestyle preferences. Soon it blended right into all the other pantheistic practices that "empower" modern feminists and holistic healers.

"The Chinese *ch'i*, the Hindu *prana*, and the Hawaiian *mana* [remember the mana song at the Re-Imagining Conference] are clearer terms for the idea of an underlying vital energy that infuses, creates, and sustains the physical body," says Starhawk.[16] This "energy is . . . central to magic. It can be molded, directed, and changed. . . . It is the basis for Chinese acupuncture and Hindu yoga, as well as psychic healings, worldwide."[17]

Energy we can mold and direct. That fits the bill. Like Tracy, feminists have found the key to power on their own terms: cosmic energy — earthy power that becomes power from within. "Goddess/me, me/Goddess." Power that will accomplish my will.

No lie pleases Satan more! He doesn't mind humoring seekers long enough to bring them into his domain. From his twisted perspective, God's good is evil, and God's evil is good. This is the message he teaches his subjects. So when women become desensitized to evil, addicted to occult thrills, and accustomed to doing their own will, they cannot see the good in God's will. Viewing life through occult lenses, they see God as their enemy and His will as cruel chains. They couldn't be more wrong.

God's Perfect Will

God loves all of us as distinct individuals. Therefore, He gave us free will. He wants us to return that love, but He doesn't force us. He tells us what is good so we can choose wisely, but it's our choice. If I choose my own way, Satan wins and I lose. If I go God's way, I win — and I find the best friend and counselor I could ever know.

Satan and his unholy armies don't hesitate to tempt, trick, or lie. Anything goes! In the battle to win new victims, they follow no rules other than their own. Neither polite nor honest, they have all the advantages when it comes to deceptive warfare. Yet, they would lose a fair battle, for their strength crumbles before God's greater might.

God doesn't force us to do anything. His will is to pour His love and life into us, to make us one with himself in an eternal love relationship — yet allow us to be ourselves. His will is our sanctification:[18] that we become holy like himself, so that nothing can separate us from Him and all He wants to give us.

But some churches no longer talk about the love relationship God offers us. They don't talk about God's solution to sin or the comfort of knowing His will. These essential truths have been squeezed out by popular demand and feel-good activities.

"Don't count on organized Christianity to combat the spread of witchcraft," said Ambrose Evans-Pritchard, a priest troubled by the spread of paganism among Catholic women. "This [religious feminism] *is* organized Christianity. The most radical wing of American feminism, it seems, is now lodged in the churches and the nunnery."[19]

These women are angry, and their number is growing fast. As in Old Testament days, it takes no more than a generation for a nation to shift its loyalties from the Shepherd who protects it to "other gods" who destroyed it. Faithful Samuel carried a sad but timely message to Saul, the first king of ancient Israel:

> Rebellion *is as* the sin of witchcraft, And stubbornness *is as* iniquity and idolatry. Because you have rejected the word of the Lord, He also has rejected you from being king (1 Sam. 15:23).

Saul had followed his feelings rather than God's Word,

therefore God could no longer use him as a leader. Soon an unholy, "distressing spirit" began to torment him, driving him to murderous fury. Only the sweet music played by the shepherd boy David could soothe his troubled mind. Having rejected God's gentle guidance, Saul faced the terrors of a demonic substitute.

"But," you might argue, "I thought God offered us freedom. How can there be freedom if I have to obey someone?"

First, remember, you *don't* have to obey. God won't force you. You can do your own thing — and face the consequences. He won't stop you.

Second, when you know the boundaries, you can choose to live within the safety He offers. There's little freedom where there's no safety. When most Americans lived by God's guidelines, our streets were safe. Children could freely bike to school and play in the dark. Today, few follow His guidelines, and individual freedom is limited by all kinds of fears. But our shrinking liberty is only a small illustration of what happens in the spiritual realm.

In Romans 1:18–32, God shows us what happens when teachers like Margie *"suppress the truth* in unrighteousness." In an insightful explanation of this passage, my pastor, Dr. Ray Stamps, shows the hidden reason for today's spreading fear, abuse, and social disintegration.

First, when people suppress the truth, they are left without a standard or reference point. Now they have no way of knowing whether they are taking the right or the wrong way. They become "unrighteous" — they don't do right — and they despise the standard that proves them wrong. All the more, they mock God's truth and vilify His way.

Look what happens next:

- *"They did not glorify Him as God, nor were thankful, but became futile in their thoughts"* (Rom. 1:21). They would think, and reason, and search in vain. Today, young girls and women are told that it's wrong to do "right," and it's right to do "what's me." Since there is no standard for "me-ness," they are confused and unsettled and have no real basis for feeling good about themselves other than psychological speculations and self-made affirmations. The "me" is never quite good enough. So they test new ideas, try new solutions, and find new gods — but get no closer to lasting peace or happiness.

- *"And their foolish hearts were darkened"* (Rom. 1:21). Their hearts, the deepest level of who they really are, can no longer see or understand reality. Having no reference points, they drift from one experience to another. In this blinding darkness, disillusionment reigns.

- *"Professing to be wise, they became fools"* (Rom. 1:22). The word for fools here *(moras)* points to a moral, not intellectual, defect. It deals with character, not ability. Degraded in heart and character, they lose all moral judgment and become unreliable and immoral.

- They *"changed the glory of the incorruptible God into an image made like corruptible man — and birds and four-footed animals and creeping things"* (Rom. 1:23). Remember, that was the purpose at the Re-Imagining Conference. The leaders tried to change the eternal God into images of created beings that decay and die. The result is a fixation on corruptible things — including self — that decay and die, followed by an endless stream of disappointment and grief.

The downward progression doesn't stop here. Three deeper and more painful consequences follow, each starting with the words: *"God gave them up (or over) to. . . ."* We'll only look at the first one here:

Therefore GOD ALSO GAVE THEM UP to uncleanness, in the lusts of their hearts, to dishonor their bodies among themselves, who exchanged the truth of God for the lie, and worshipped and served the creature rather than the Creator, who is blessed forever (Rom. 1: 24–25).

When people reject God, they lose more than the warmth of His presence. He "gives them over" to who they really are. Left to their own resources and Satan's schemes, they face the driving force of their own desires. The more they feed their wants, the more cravings increase. Following that insatiable nature, they violate the natural order established by God, but run further away from the only source of lasting help.

There is no freedom for those who are controlled by their wants. The next two chapters will show why. Those who have struggled with addictions to alcohol, drugs, food, or even shopping can testify to our human resistance to doing right. No one described that struggle better than Paul:

What I am doing, I do not understand. For what I will to do, that I do not practice; but what I hate, that I do. . . . To will is present with me, but *how* to perform what is good I do not find. For the good that I will *to do*, I do not do; but the evil I will *not to do,* that I practice (Rom. 7:15–19).

Everything changed when Paul joined his inadequate will to God's perfect will. His desire became God's desire, and God's strength became his strength. But those whose minds have been blinded by today's spiritual alternatives cannot see the difference. Chapter 5 shows what happens next.

Endnotes

[1] Sonia Johnson, "Women, Desire and History," *Woman of Power,* Spring 1990, p. 73.

[2] Starhawk, *The Spiral Dance* (San Francisco, CA: Harper & Row Publishers, 1979), p. 124.

[3] This statement will probably raise more questions that cannot be answered briefly. I deal with some environmental issues in chapter 9, and many more in my book *Brave New Schools.* For a scholarly exposé on environmental issues by nationally respected scientists, I recommend *The True State of the Planet,* edited by Ronald Bailey (New York, NY: The Free Press, 1995).

[4] Philippians. 2:5–11.

[5] 1 John 5:14–15

[6] Starhawk, *The Spiral Dance*, p. 124.

[7] Legalistic churches make rules and set standards not taught in God's Word. They demand obedience based on human strength, not the sufficiency of Christ in a believer. Therefore, they produce failure and disillusionment. Only the exchanged life described in Galatians 2:20 can fulfill God's standards.

[8] Ntozake Shange, Re-Imagining Conference, tape 2-1, side A.

[9] Galatians 1:8-9; Revelation 22:19; Acts 17:11; Deuteronomy 4:2, 12:32; Proverbs 30:6.

[10] Starhawk, *The Spiral Dance*, p. 142.

[11] Starhawk, *Dreaming the Dark* (Boston, MA: Beacon Press, 1988), p. 49.

[12] Starhawk, *The Spiral Dance,* p. 62

[13] Deuteronomy 18:9-12.

[14] Ari L. Goldman, "Religious Notes," *The New York Times*, January 1, 1991.

[15] Starhawk, *Dreaming the Dark*, 51

[16] Ibid.

[17] Ibid., p. 52.

[18] 1 Thessalonians 4:3.

[19] Ambrose Evans-Pritchard, "Every Witch Way to the Goddess," *The Sunday Telegraph* (Mankato, Minnesota), October 17, 1993.

Chapter 5

Give Us... Daily Bread, or Don't Give! I Own?

❦

To return to worship the goddess as sacred female is to reconnect with our own deep powers.[1] (Rosemary Reuther, The Renaissance of Christian Spirituality)

You live in an abundant universe, in which you can co-create resources by the power of thought.... Your thought will utterly control the vibrations of the light waves which are your body.[2] (Barbara Marx Hubbard, *Revelation*)

When a woman has owned her passionate nature... her thoughts grow wild and fierce and beautiful.... She has thrown off crutch and ... glimpsed the enchanted kingdom, the vast and magical realms of the Goddess within her.[3] (Marianne Williamson)

I am the bread of life. He who comes to Me shall never hunger, and he who believes in Me shall never thirst. (Jesus — John 6:35)

༄

A new store has opened in our little suburban downtown. I first noticed it in a newspaper list of local classes. "Women's mysteries, Rituals and Initiation," it said. Then one day, coming out of Peet's Coffee shop, I noticed the sign: Phoenix Earth Store. I stopped and prayed, then stepped into an occult fantasy world of fragrant incense, tinkling waterfalls, and mystical music as ethereal as the airbrushed pastel-colored mural on the nearest wall. Around me hung pictures that ranged from sweet animal photographs to eerie paintings of wolf-like spirits hovering over shape-shifting shamans, spiritual mediators who could appear as wolf or man, buffalo or woman.

The shelves were lined with beautiful rocks, crystals, and candles — the kind anyone would enjoy in a less intimidating context. More obviously occult were the wizards, crescent moons, and goddess figures. "It looks like a museum," commented another first-time visitor.

Several women of all ages (no men) were browsing among the bookshelves. I joined them and scanned some of the titles: *Dance of Power, A Shamanic Journey, The Circle is Sacred. . . .*

All offer tempting counterfeits to God's promises, I thought. *Do these women have any idea where these paths would lead?*

I asked a middle-aged woman which book she had found most helpful. She pulled down a pink-and-purple paperback titled *Healing Yourself with Light: How to Connect with Angelic Healers.*

"This one," she said, handing it to me.

I turned it over and read the back cover. Apparently, this book taught *"a* method for bringing the healing light of the Solar Angel and the angelic healers into the physical body."[4]

"I have a guardian angel," she volunteered.

"Does it help you?"

"Yes," she answered. "Actually I have more than one. They encourage me and keep me centered."

I wanted to ask more questions, but the woman left. I replaced the angel book, picked up *Phoenix Rising* by Mary Summer Rain, and opened it. It invited me to "join in engineering a new harmonious world based upon the beautiful foundation of God's Golden Light."

That "Golden Light" could *not* belong to the God I know. Instead it fit into a grandiose vision that would transform nations, renew its people, and make us all one — *just what God warned us would happen.*

At the counter was a tray of rocks decorated with animal drawings. "What are those?" I asked the woman.

"Animal Energy Stones," she answered with a friendly smile. "They bring whatever energy you need for the day. Center yourself, then pick out one that feels good to you."

"One that feels good? They all look about the same."

"Or just close your eyes and let the stone pick you."

"How do you do that?"

"Three girls came in here yesterday. They're just 14 and they're really into this. One girl closed her eyes, and picked out the same stone three times. *It* chose her.

"Either that, or ..." she picked up a small pink card with tiny letters on it, "look at this card and find the animal strength you need today. Here's a snake." She held out a flat gray rock with a snake drawing. "That means life force and sexual energy. And," she picked another, "this little bear stone will bring physical strength."

"What are these?" I pointed to a bowl of little leather pouches. "Are they medicine pouches for the energy stones?"

"That's right."

I thanked her for her help and bought a book for my research. On the way out I scanned the bench covered with free brochures and pamphlets announcing Wiccan events and workshops. "Allow the safety of a circle of women to cradle you as you explore what it means to be a strong woman, a wild woman, a passionate woman," suggested the leader of a program called Tantra for Women. "Universal energy gives you exactly what you need and desire at that moment," promised someone who teaches the Language of Light.

I shuddered, hurried out, and took a deep breath of fresh, unscented air. The Phoenix Earth Store may offer fascinating thrills to women seeking mystical insight, but to me it was oppressive. "Thank You, my Lord," I whispered, "for showing me the true light. I could so easily have been one of those women."

As always, the lures of the occult promise what our human nature wants: self-discovery, self-healing, self-empowerment, self-determination. You *own* your body, your mind, your destiny. *You* direct the energies of nature. Visualize what *you* want — and go for it!

Women who believe the lies don't need to ask God for anything — not His gifts, nor His strength, nor His life. Believing they "own" their source of physical and spiritual sustenance, they scorn the "the living bread which came down from heaven." Who needs to feed on the life of Jesus, when loving angels and cosmic forces are as available as a genie in a lamp? Why follow His teaching, when the passions of the body create more energy and immediate delights?

I thought of David, God's beloved shepherd-king. "Help, Lord," he prayed in Psalm 12. Sad that his people would trade God's infinite strength for an illusion of human self-sufficiency, he continued, "May the Lord cut off all flattering lips and the tongue that speaks proud things, who have said, 'With our tongue we will prevail; Our lips *are* our own; Who *is* lord over us?' "

"Eros, Ecstasy, and Creation."

The title of Grace Cathedral's 1995 conference on "Christian spirituality" promised lots of fleshly delights but little biblical wisdom. Waiting in line, once again, outside San Francisco's massive Episcopal cathedral, I read the conference program:

> The Renaissance of Christian Spirituality restores the original splendor of Christ's vision: the Divine Eros linking the soul with God. . . . Restoring this original passion is crucial for the embodiment of sacred wisdom and the essential transformation of consciousness needed to preserve the planet.

The church doors opened and the crowd began to press forward. At the entrance, a woman handed me a program.

"How many do you expect?" I asked her.

"About eight hundred," she answered.

Someone announced that books were for sale in the back of the church. I went to look, and noticed a large book by futurist Barbara Marx Hubbard titled *Revelation*. I picked it up, opened it to a page near the center and read a paragraph that began, "Godly children always know they are about God's business."

The words sounded Christian, but the context was occult. The next sentence left no doubt about the source: "You will be capable of self-healing, telepathy, clairvoyance, clairaudience. . . . Empathetic love will be a constant state. A community of natural Christs attuning to the design of God . . . suprasexually engaged in conscious co-creation, ever ecstatic, ever new, ever mindful of God."[5]

What a confusing blend of Christian words and occult concepts. A quick survey showed that Barbara Marx Hubbard, or her "inner voice," had reinterpreted the entire Book of Revelation, piece by piece — everything except chapter 17 which shows both the return and the destruction of the pagan Babylonian prostitute. The "voice" seemed to be a spirit that called itself Christ. I prayed for the protection only the true Christ can give, then read on.

> You will be androgynous. You will learn to
> co-create. . . . You will choose to create another
> being only on very special occasions when the
> whole community of natural Christs sees the
> requirement. . . . You produce as God does. You
> heal as God does. . . .[6]

Was she saying that new babies would only be born when the whole community agreed? That seemed a strange contradiction to the feminist demand that each woman own her own body and control her own productivity. It even clashed with her own claim that anyone could be a "natural Christ," empowered to create, produce, and heal "as God does." Yet, it fit the collective political ideals of radical feminists. Thus, on the one hand, no one would need to ask God for anything, since people would have the power of god. On the other hand, each individual god would have to bow to the collective god — the "community of natural Christs!"

"That's the best book I've ever read," said the woman next to me.

I turned to her and smiled. "What makes it so good?"

She thought for a moment. "It's about transformation. It's about hope for the future. Our collective minds evolving together toward a new unity."

When I handed it to the saleswoman, another woman spoke up. "You're going to love that book."

A deep haunting sound began to fill the cavernous cathedral, driving us to our seats. It sounded like some kind of horn. On the stage built over the church altar, someone was blowing into one end of a long uneven tube. The other end rested on a pedestal. The strange instrument, I read in the program, was a didgeridoo, a Eucalyptus tree hollowed by termites and traditionally played by Australian aborigines. Its owner, Stephen Kent, swayed and curved like a cobra dancing to the tune of a Hindu piper. As the eerie, monotonous sound droned on, I instinctively wanted to shut it out, to cover my ears — anything to escape the tremulous sounds.

Nature as Guide

When the haunting sounds finally melted into the opening chords of a grand organ, the dean of the cathedral, Alan Jones, walked to the podium. "There are many voices of Christians in this culture," he began, "and it's time the voices represented here are heard." He introduced Lauren Artress and Robert McDermott as "two great friends and lovers of Christ." Reverend Artress, director of Quest, Grace Cathedral Center for Spiritual Wholeness, spoke first.

"There is indeed a renaissance of Christian spirituality," she began. "It's taking on momentum. This is coming in through practices that are coming back into Christianity — the methods, the way of meditation, the labyrinth. . . . We want to once again discover our path. . . . Our three themes that we begin to weave together this evening are Eros — the whole sense of love, love for the divine, for our bodies, for ourselves. . . . The second is Ecstasy . . . a lost thread, the sense of blissing out on God, being so full of love and divine that you are ecstatic. . . . The last is Creation. . . . We acknowledge that we have to have a larger story than we have had in the past — a story that unites us and incorporates the whole cosmos."[7]

What an enticing mix, I thought. *Who wouldn't want to be "blissing out on God" while writing one's own imaginary story about God and His cosmos.*

Apparently, in this world of imagined innocence and bliss, the animal spirit within would be free to speak. We would "go out and howl with our own voices," said Paul Winter, composer of the controversial Missa Gaia musical, which blends the trumpeting of elephants, the howling of wolves, and the sounds of the dolphin into a symphony of praise to mother earth. "We, as a much younger species, would learn something from these elders of ours."

"Wolves are not dangerous to man,"[8] he assured us. "Join me in a hallelujah chorus by howling like wolves." Moments later, the cavernous cathedral reverberated with chilling imitations of howling wolves — some called it a "Howl-eluia chorus."

"When I fall on my knees, with my face to the rising sun . . ." sang the Oakland Interfaith Gospel Choir moments later.

O Lord, have mercy on us! I had heard that song many times in traditional churches, and it always disturbed me. My mind drifted to pagan cultures where priests or shamans lead their tribes in worship to the rising sun.[9]

"I will go in Jesus' name," sang the Interfaith Choir. "I'll spread the gospel in Jesus name. . . ."

"O Jesus," I whispered, "I'm afraid most of these people don't even know You."

Earthy Powers

The next day, the conference moved to the Star King Unitarian-Universalist Church. Rosemary Reuther, professor of theology at the Garette-Evangelical Theological Seminary (United Methodist) in Evanston, Illinois, spoke first. At first glance, her grandmotherly appearance disguised her pagan dreams and impressive titles: theologian, scholar, educator, visionary, and revolutionary.

"Feminism," she began, "is a complex movement." She listed some of its "many layers" and demands:

> • Full inclusion of women in political rights.
> • Access to full employment.
> • Transformation of the patriarchal socio-economic system in which male domination of woman is the foundation of social hierarchies.

Few would disagree with the first two,[10] but the third and more basic demand requires a total transformation of western culture. Never mind that eastern cultures are far less friendly to feminist ideals than their western counterparts. (Just look at China, Japan, and Iran.) The spiritual master-mind behind this movement has aimed his bullets at Judeo-Christian monotheism (one God), not Eastern monism (all is one). In his grandiose plan, injustice toward women is merely an excuse for vilifying Christian influences. He couldn't care less about wounded women.

Small wonder then, that feminists seek far more than equality. They call for a revolution — a new culture, a new history, new government, a new form of global socialism, and a new religion. The new religion is essential because, according to Reuther and other feminists, the old "patriar-chal religions" caused all the problems in the first place.

"The Western ruling class male," explained Rosemary Reuther, "made God in his own image — or rather in the image of his aspiration." Her answer to male domination echoes what the leaders of the Re-imagining Conference declared: Women must create *their* own deity — one that reflects *their* image and aspirations and brings them back in touch with the earth:

> There are deep, positive connections be-tween women and nature. Women are the life givers, the nurturers, the ones in whom the seed of life grows. Women were the primary food gather-ers, the inventors of agriculture. Their bodies are in mysterious tune with the cycles of the moon. The tides of the sea. And it was by experiencing women as life givers, both food providers and "birthers" of children, that the early human com-munities in fact made the female the first image of worship, the goddess, the source of all life.[11]

"Women need to reclaim this affinity between the 'sacrality' of nature and the 'sacrality' of their own sexuality and life powers," she continued. "To return to worship the goddess as sacred female is to reconnect with our own deep powers."

Our own deep powers? The tragedy is that Reuther and other would-be historians are telling a lie. The women they present as models didn't exist. Earth-centered women never did have the powers today's feminist envision. The bane and blessing of the imagination is that you don't have to prove anything. The fact is that ancient women or indigenous women would beg their various gods and spirit for the food and protection we now take for granted. They lived at the mercy of the spirits from whom they bought favors they desperately needed. Indigenous people are still tormented by the spirits they fear.[12]

The goddess figures archeologists have uncovered are less a testimony to the power of women than a sign of the superstitions that dominated their lives. In pagan cultures, sacrificial offerings helped pay capricious spirits or demons for basic needs: a fertile harvest, food for the family, a baby. Fighting life-and-death battles against disease, curses, tempestuous weather, and wild animals, people had little time to seek self-esteem, self-sufficiency, and *control* over their own life and body. A good year meant food to eat, and a child that didn't die. Well aware that their lives were driven by forces they could not control, they would plead and appease, not command.

Barbara Marx Hubbard, who followed Reuther, also promised imagined power — but with a New Age twist. Instead of a goddess, her story points to a more impersonal New Age force. Like so many others, she cloaks her occult ideas in Christian terms and puts Scriptures into a pagan context:

> In the sixties I began reading Teillard deChardin. What is interesting about Teillard is that the evolution of our planet leads to a time on earth which he calls Omega. . . . Our system, as it becomes more complex, is rising in conscious-

ness, and at some point he felt there would be a quantum jump in which we would empathetically experience ourselves as connected to the whole. . . . I related it to reading in the Bible, "Behold I tell you a mystery. We shall not all sleep, we shall all be changed, in a moment, in a twinkling of an eye."

> I had an experience of the . . . field of light . . . it had persona and it was real. . . . I felt enfolded in light and I heard the words, "My resurrection was real. It is a forecast of what you will do collectively when you love God above all else, your neighbor as yourself, yourself as me, a natural Christ. . . . You shall all be changed. . . ."

When the "inner voice" spoke to Ms. Hubbard's heart, she sensed "an overwhelming magnetic love."[13] In silence, she replied, "I choose it, but I don't know how to do it."

Again "the presence" spoke. "You choose it. I'll do it."

This exchange began her relationship with "a Being" that has produced books, lectures, and countless followers who continue to spread the illusion of abundant life through a counterfeit Christ.

The "Christ" who spoke to Barbara Marx Hubbard promised a massive change when the global consciousness has reached what many call a "critical mass." In her book, she talks about a violent "planetary birth experience" when the "ancient defect of consciousness" will "be corrected forever."[14] At that point — "when enough of you are attracted and linked"[15] — her Christ would return, but not in person as will the true Christ. Instead his "presence" (his spirit or glory) would appear and draw all people into an ultimate universal humanity.

If this occult "Christ" who pulls people to himself with "overwhelming love" — and will one day appear as a mystical "presence" — sounds like a movement within churches today, you have reason to be concerned. Remember, Satan twists all of God's good things into tempting counterfeits that lure people toward himself.

I Own My Body

"You will be in charge of your body," the Christ spirit told Barbara Marx Hubbard, "maintaining it, discarding it, or evolving it into new forms."[16]

Her "Christ" has prophesied the coming of "uncontrollable joy" which will "ripple through the thinking layers of the earth." It will be as "irresistible as sex," flooding all human "co-creative systems" with "love and attraction."[17]

Who will "awaken this co-creative" genius and prepare the world for "the Second Coming?"

"The Holy Spirit," says Hubbard's Christ.[18] But humans have to help, and this is where Hubbard's evolutionary force joins contemporary neo-paganism. To help you evolve, Hubbard suggests standard circle rituals: create a sacred space, light candles, and pass the sacred wine or juice. There Hubbard would "evoke the presence of the living Christ"[19] instead of the Wiccan goddess, but as you know, the label matters little. For more practical helps, she suggests *A Course in Miracles* — the occult messages channeled by a spirit guide and taught by Marrianne Williamson, guru to Hollywood and Oprah Winfrey.[20]

Do you see the common threads that link all the diverse pagan groups? Do you wonder why God warns us that "false Christs and false prophets will rise and show great signs and wonders to deceive, if possible, even the elect"? Or why He tells us to "test the spirits?"[21]

The high-brow spirituality of Barbara Marx Hubbard may contrast sharply with the naked sensuality of the new rage: the "wild" women who join circle covens or worship the goddess in forested groves. But the difference is superficial. In essence, both forms of occultism spring from the same spiritual source. Both promise love, super sex, ownership of one's own body, and answers to personal needs and wants. Anything goes, no matter how outrageous.

"Snake Power is power from within," says Vicki Noble, a feminist and shamanic healer. "Snake Power is moving us toward global female leadership. A woman with Snake Power stands her ground, allowing the fires of transformation to boil up in her and direct her actions."[22]

Who then directs her actions?

You may remember Annie Sprinkle. She stirred quite a commotion some years ago when *your* taxes helped pay for *her* obscene video. An earlier live performance had featured Sprinkle chanting prayers to the "spirits of ancient sacred temple prostitutes" and inviting her audience to examine her private parts. The ecstatic Annie then uttered the immortal line, *"Usually I get paid a lot of money for this, but tonight it's government funded."*[23]

More recently she performed at the Wild Wise Woman Center, "a safe space for restoring the health, wholeness, and holiness of women . . . where women can explore the deep wellsprings of female power."

Annie called her show Sacred Sex. "Explore sexual energy as a vehicle for enlightenment and healing," beckoned her ad. "Learn Tantric, Taoist, and Native American techniques. . . . Explore the mysteries of the sacred slut. Oh yes."

Once again the world's religions are blending together in a universal expression of the untamed self: the wild woman. The *Wise Woman Center Gazette* describes her well. It defines *wild* as "free, untamed, not under man's domination, virgin."

The wild woman is a virgin? Yes, for "virgin" has also been redefined. Carol Christ, former associate professor of Women's Studies and Religious Studies at San Jose State University, gives her version in her book, *Laughter of Aphrodite.* She writes:

> Fully and joyously sexual, Aphrodite remains virgin in that her sexuality is *unbridled,*

untamed, and *her own.* Though married to Hephaestus . . . she is neither submissive or faithful to him. Though she is a mother, her child Eros, Love or Desire, is but a reflection of her sexuality.[24] (Emphasis added)

Aphrodite also represents the "cosmic life force, associated especially with the transformative power of sexuality."

So does the goddess in Marianne Williamson's popular books. "Like every aspect of the cosmic energy of which she is a part," writes the famous author, "she permeates the cells of those who have invited her in. She gives us new life, that we might give it to others. Through her power within us, we redeem all things."[25]

Ponder the above sentence. If "we redeem all things," there's no need for Jesus and His gifts. If "our life is our kingdom,"[26] there's no need for His life. And if women accept her lie that it is good to "grow wild and fierce" by "owning their passionate nature," they will surely hate the Cross which frees us from bondage to that capricious nature.

Like Barbara Marx Hubbard, Ms. Williamson often refers to a Christ who opposes everything the Bible teaches. This twisted message made her a rising star on the television circuit and a welcome overnight guest at the Hillary Clinton White House.[27] Few seem to care that her message was channeled by a spirit guide and first packaged as *A Course in Miracles.*

"If we truly believed in an internal light, we . . . would not be so easy to dominate and control," says Williamson, bringing us full circle back to Grace Cathedral and the cosmic force behind its "Renaissance of Christian Spirituality: Eros, Ecstasy and Creation." She is wrong. The next three chapters will show that the deeper the journey into the occult, the stronger is the domination. Women may visualize a sweet, lovely goddess, but her dark side is cruel beyond the imagination of our still-civilized Western world. It may take little more than a generation to revive the basic depravity of pagan wildness. No longer tempered by Judeo-Christian civility, it will soon be free to express itself in all its natural fury.

That's hard to believe in today's politically correct atmosphere. Blinded by noble educational sentiments, we don't want to consider the fact that certain earth-centered cultures were destructive both to its human victims and its land. Missionaries saw the pain of occult bondage and scientists have documented the erosion and pollution that followed destructive lifestyles, but those are secrets well-hidden from the general public. Instead we learn from Disney's Pocahontas and Lion King which tell us the new-paradigm version of history — the one that will raise our consciousness and usher in the new paradigm world.

The lie is believable because it sounds so good. You want self-esteem? Self-knowledge? Listen to Starhawk who has a way of turning the old-paradigm evils into new-paradigm virtues. "Witchcraft is a religion of self-celebration," she writes in *The Spiral Dance.* "Desire is the glue of the universe. . . . So fulfillment becomes, not a matter of self-indulgence, but of self-*awareness.*"[28]

Witchcraft looks good to women who equate their natural desires with social virtues. Symbolic art, simplified lifestyles, and environmental concern blend with sexual freedom and the dream of power. Together they draw seekers who are rightly offended by today's blatant consumerism. But the promising paths lead to disillusionment and bondage, for Satan never lets his human victims *own* his power. Remember, he who masquerades as an "angel of light"[29] said to Barbara Marx Hubbard, "You choose. I will do it." He may use a long leash, but — whether his victims know it or not — he, not they, holds the reel.

Most of them don't know. That's part of the scheme.

Give Us This Day. . . .

Feminists accuse Christianity of stirring "hostility toward sexual pleasure."[30] That's a lie. God invented both sex and pleasure. Satan can only twist what God has given for our delight. He takes God's greatest gifts — motherhood, a beautiful sunrise, a new spiritual insight, sexual enjoyment — and perverts them into lures that bring social and personal destruction.

In every battle between the two opposing spiritual forces, God wins hands down. Satan is only a created being, and God holds his leash. But He won't win the battle for those who twist His truths and dance with His enemy. Caught in the awesome slide described in Romans 1, they become victims of the very desires they feed.

You saw the new definition for the wild woman. Actually, the *Wild Woman Center Gazette* gave a second list of meanings: "Wild is 'unruly, abandoned, full of chaos, lunatic.' Like a wild animal, like a river at flood...." In other words, turbulent, raging, destructive, and deadly. That's what we see in Romans 1:18-27. Remember the downward progression that begins when people "suppress the truth," so that they can't tell right from wrong?

- They become futile in their thoughts.
- Their foolish hearts are darkened.
- Professing to be wise, they become fools.

Three more devastating results follow. Each starts with the words: *"God gave them up to . . ."* indicating that God pulled back His needed resources and left them — both individually and collectively — to face their capricious human nature. You saw the first one at the end of chapter 4. Here is the second one:

> For this reason GOD GAVE THEM UP to vile passions. For even their women exchanged the natural use for what is against nature. Likewise also the men . . . burned in their lust for one another, men with men committing what is shameful, and receiving in themselves the penalty of

their error which was due (Rom. 1:26-27).

All kinds of personal struggles, obsessions, addictions, and misery can be explained simply by understanding what happens when people turn from God to the seductions of paganism. Unlike God who loves us, Satan loves no one, nor does he hesitate to inspire and energize the worst in human nature — with the agonizing results we will look at in the next two chapters.

Oswald Chambers said it well:

"If I enthrone anything other than God in my life,
God retires and lets the other god do what it can."

Endnotes

[1]Rosemary Reuther speaking at the San Francisco conference, "Eros, Ecstasy and Creation: A Renaissance of Christian Spirituality," March 25,1995.

[2]Barbara Marx Hubbard, *Revelation* (Greenbrae, CA: The Foundation for Conscious Evolution), 111-112.

[3]Marianne Williamson, *A Woman's Worth* (New York: Ballantine Books, 1993), 11.

[4]Launa Huffines, Healing Yourself with Light (Tiburon, CA: H.J. Kramer, Inc., 199); back cover.

[5]Hubbard, 154. Her interpretation of Revelations 10:5-7.

[6]Ibid., 154-155.

[7]Renaissance of Christian Spirituality Conference, March 24, 1995. Transcribed from tape.

[8]This is not true, as Finn's and Norwegians know well. Allowed to freely multiply, at the cost of ranch animals and children's safety, the wolves in Wyoming may soon prove less friendly than their friendly photographs suggest. (See Jeremiah 5:6; Matthew 7:15; Acts 20:29)

[9]John 6:35, 48. Sun worship characterized ancient Middle Eastern, Egyptian, and Roman civilizations as well as Indo-European, Meso-American, and some Native American cultures. In their pantheon of gods and spirits, the sun god reigned supreme as the all-seeing all-powerful source of life and wisdom. He usually required human sacrifice.

[10]On the surface, the first two points seem generally acceptable, but some of the feminist interpretations involve deeper implications

with regard to workplace quotas, gender education, and change in social consciousness.

[11]Rosemary Radford Ruether, "Healing Violence to Creation," a keynote address given at the Renaissance of Christian Spirituality Conference, March 25, 1995.

[12]Mission stories about demon oppression and curses.

[13]Hubbard, *Revelation,* 75.

[14]Ibid., 242.

[15]Ibid., 62.

[16]Ibid., 92.

[17]Ibid., 234.

[18]Ibid., 287.

[19]Ibid., 313.

[20]Ibid., 335.

[21]Matthew 24:23-24 and 1 John 4:1.

[22]Schedule of events, *Wise Woman Center Gazette*, February 17, 1994.

[23]James F. Cooper, "Art Censors: A Closer Look at the NEA," *New Dimensions* (June 1991): 26.

[24]Carol P. Christ, *Laughter of Aphrodite* (San Francisco: Harper & Row, 1987), 176-177.

[25]Williamson, 33.

[26]Ibid., 10.

[27]Leah Garchik, "Personals," *San Francisco Chronicle*, December 20, 1994.

[28]Starhawk, *The Spiral Dance* (San Francisco: Harper & Row, 1979), 99.

[29]2 Cor. 11:14.

[30]Sara Solovitch, "New book links sex to religion," *San Jose Mercury News*, July 29, 1995.

Chapter 6

Forgive Us . . . as We Forgive, or I Choose to Forgive or Curse?

❧

> *I had a lot of negative feelings to try to dissipate. My forgiveness chant — a kind of mantra, or repeated affirmation of spiritual wisdom — worked like a healing balm on my emotional turmoil.* (Marianne Williamson in *A Return to Love*)[1]

> *Kali manifested herself for the annihilation of demonic male power in order to restore peace and equilibrium. For a long time asuric (demonic) forces had been dominating and oppressing the world.* (Manuela Dunn Mascetti)[2]

> *Forgive, and you will be forgiven.* (Luke 6:37-38)

❧

When Rachel Holm walked into her son's Sunday school classroom, she found a new poster on the wall. "Gathering into the Sacred Circle," it said. Surprised, she stopped to look at the symbol under the words. It showed a cross inside a circle — but it didn't quite look like the Christian cross. Could it be the medicine wheel — an occult symbol used by Native Americans in many of their rituals? Her heart began to pound. Why would a Lutheran Sunday school curriculum use this symbol?

Moments later she saw her pastor, so she asked him. He seemed reluctant to answer, but indicated that in today's pluralistic culture, Christians must be open to new ideas. What did he mean? Rachel felt confused.

Curious, she ordered the manual describing the curriculum called "The Whole People of God" from a distributor for Augsburg Publishing House. She learned that it was being used by more than a thousand congregations from coast to coast, including most mainstream denominations: Presbyterian, Methodist, Lutheran, United Church of Christ, etc. "Sales are booming," said the telephone representative.

When she received the manual, Rachel noticed that matching lessons were prepared for each age group — from young children to adults. It also explained the poster she first saw in her son's classroom: "The logo for Unit I is a circle symbolizing God and the interconnection of the whole creation." Concerned, Rachel read on:

> The center that keeps the circle together may be called Creator or Great Spirit, or God. The circle in our logo is made with braided sweetgrass which is used by many people of the First Nations to purify or cleanse the body and soul. . . .[3]

Did it imply that cleansing came through the Native American sweetgrass ritual, and not through Jesus Christ? What about confession and repentance? Rachel turned the page and found an unexpected answer to her question: an "apology to Native Congregations" submitted by the United Church of Canada in 1986. Sad, she read the words to the strange confession:

> In our zeal to tell you of the good news of Jesus Christ we were closed to the value of your spirituality. . . .
>
> We tried to make you be like us and in so doing we helped to destroy the vision that made you what you were.
>
> As a result you, and we, are poorer and the image of the Creator in us is twisted, blurred. . . .
>
> We ask you to forgive us . . . .[4]

"This is a politically correct Sunday school curriculum," Rachel told me later. "Christian children learn that they are guilty simply because they are part of a culture that taught others to trust Jesus Christ. It tells our children that it's *wrong* to be missionaries, but *right* to blend Christianity with Native American spirituality or any other pantheistic religion."

New Grounds for Forgiveness

Rachel knew the Bible well enough to see the gulf between God's truth and today's new standards. Some prefer not to look. As you will see in chapter 8, many feminists reject the concept of sin altogether. Others sense a need to confess *something* in order to feel forgiven, but they have never learned what God considers right or wrong. To them, it doesn't really matter. Admitting what *they* believe is wrong soothes their sense of guilt and dulls their sensitivity to God's view of sin.

Sin means "missing the mark" — God's mark. Those who don't read His Word, won't see that "mark." Certain to miss it, they aim for a different kind of mark, one easier to hit. For some, the new mark might be the new politically correct standards. Many find it far more comfortable to confess a corporate sin such as *cultural sexism* or *intolerance* than to disturb their own comfort zone by facing embarrassing personal sins such as envy or immorality.[5]

Actually, public confession need not be embarrassing

at all. These days it can even help your public image, raise self-esteem, and bring lots of warm hugs and affirmations. It can show others your willingness to be open and vulnerable, to express your feelings, and to conform to the new group norms . . . all of which are essential to the new-paradigm community. From *its* perspective, the best kinds of confession are those that affirm the evils of the old ways and the ideals of the new quest for pluralistic oneness.

Such a confession was suggested by former World Council of Churches President Lois Wilson at the Re-Imagining Conference:

> Can we re-imagine an apology by the institutional churches to the aboriginal people for collapsing their culture, their spirituality, their language, and abusing their children in residential schools?[6]

"Abusing their children" meant teaching them to read and follow the Bible. This promotion of "classism" — the belief that *your* ways and values might be better than others — is intolerable to those who promote feminist unity. It clashes with their new moral freedom. Today's re-imagined freedom allowed lesbian leaders at the Minnesota conference to elevate their homosexual lifestyle to a divine model for perfect love. On the other hand, it condemned those who still clung to biblical guidelines such as 1 Corinthians 6:9-11: "Do not be deceived. Neither fornicators, nor idolaters, nor adulterers, nor homosexuals, nor sodomites. . . . will inherit the kingdom of God. And such were some of you. But you were washed, but you were sanctified, but you were justified in the name of the Lord Jesus and by the Spirit of our God."

The goddess Sophia fit the new mindset. "She does not judge," says Lutheran reporter Kathy Kersten, "nor does she recognize any sin but the corporate transgressions of racism, sexism, and classism. She only gives one command: 'Freely bless your own experience.' "[7]

As feminists distance themselves more and more from Christian guidelines, confession becomes increasingly mystical, feeling-centered, and occult. "Visualize a source of light about six inches above your head," suggests Ayya Khema, a German-born Buddhist. "Confess — to yourself, to the light — something you've done wrong. . . . Feel deep regret for your action. Vow not to repeat it. Experience the light above you streaming down through the crown of your head and flowing through your body, pushing out the impurities caused by action; feel the negative residue leave your body. . . . Sincerely wish that others can benefit from this light."[8]

The following counterfeit confession by Patricia Eagle is simply an upside down accusation. Instead of admitting a sin, she subtly blames the culture that caused her problems in the first place. She ends with the typical Wiccan decree, "So be it!"

> We confess that we have all been captive to the masculine mystique. . . . We confess that we have only begun to understand how much damage we have done to ourselves and to each other under the sway of this mystique. Allowing our gender to define and limit our possibilities, we have disowned those qualities and needs and feelings in ourselves which do not fit. . . . We confess that we stand in need of cleansing in order that we might experience healing and wholeness. So be it.[9]

Women as Victims

Patricia Eagle's anger typifies our victim-centered world. These are angry times. "Anger has become the national habit," observes *New York Times* columnist Russell Baker. Indigenous people are angry. Third World nations are angry. People of color are angry. White people are angry. But few groups are *more* angry than today's feminists.

In a dramatic display of feminist fury, groups of college women funded by a Presbyterian Women's Ministry Unit recite a new litany: "We will channel our rage to end the war against women! The energy of this rage empowers us to act!"[10]

The training packet supposedly used for college evangelism "reflects the feminist strategy of indoctrinating women through 'consciousness raising' sessions designed to generate anger toward men in general," explains Sue Cyre in her article, "College Women's Packet Promotes Goddess Worship." This "anger is then channeled by group leaders into actions furthering the feminist agenda."[11]

With a little help from feminist friends like Marianne Williamson, the rage spreads fast. Remember, her network of admirers include Oprah Winfrey, Hillary Clinton, and countless Hollywood stars. In her book, *A Woman's Worth,* she tells us:

> One of the most sophisticated, insidious conspiracies has been perpetrated against women. . . . Archaeological evidence now argues for the existence of a twenty-thousand-year period of history when men and women lived as equals. . . . Women were revered as priestesses and healers. . . . We healed one another through our compassionate connection to spirit and earth.
>
> The world is currently set up according to masculine models of thought and structure, and it has been for thousands of years. Aggression, force, domination, and control have been at the heart of our social agreements. Organization, technology, and rational analysis have been the order . . . [while] the feminine principles of nonviolence and the values of intuition, nurturing, and healing were pushed aside. . . .[12]
>
> The Goddess awakens in our hearts before she awakens in the world.[13]

Be careful what you believe. The "archeological evidence" she claims as proof doesn't exist outside the feminist imagination and the books it conceived. Many claim that the discovery of hundreds of early European female figurines provided the "archeological evidence" feminists needed to back their beliefs. But in the absence of cultural facts or historical data, one can only speculate. Do fertility idols, many of which showed exaggerated sexual characteristics, really prove the existence of a matriarchal culture as many feminists declare? Do they even prove equality? Or do they merely prove a reliance on pagan fertility goddesses for sun, rain, abundant fields, and fertile women? The writings of most respected scientists discount the feminist claims.

In the above quote, did you notice that Williamson, like other feminist leaders, spurns "rational analysis"? Yet, without it, genuine science can't exist. Yes, women were priestesses and healers, and we will look at those roles in the two next chapters. But their cultures were neither peaceful nor compassionate, and the ancient goddesses that modeled womanhood and power were downright scary.

So why do feminists love them? Could it be because these idols were angry, tough, and mean? Whatever the reason, many of the violent goddesses were worshiped during a 1995 chapel service at the United Methodist Garette-Evangelical Theological Seminary in Illinois. In his response to the event, faculty member Dr. Robert Jewett decried "the adoration of brutal deities" and described several. Ponder the nature of Anath "the Canaanite goddess of fertility with a thirst for violence:"

> Her mating with Baal regenerates the cycle of nature. She appears . . . as the violent sister of Baal [incest was no big deal] in the wars against the other gods, joyously riding a warhorse with blood up to its belly from victims she has dispatched. In the description of the *Anchor Bible*

Dictionary, "Anath is depicted as a fierce, invincible warrior, slaughtering people, tying their heads and hands to her person, wading knee deep in the blood and gore of those she has slain, reveling in fighting and destruction."[14]

The speaker at this chapel service was the much-quoted theologian Dr. Rosemary Ruether, who is also a faculty member at Garette-Evangelical. Naturally, she wrote a response to Dr. Jewett suggesting that he consider the "legacy of war and violence in Hebrew Scripture and Christianity."[15]

I am sure he has. Every Christian who studies history can only grieve over the atrocities that have been committed in the name of God by people who refuse to follow His ways. We see it today. Many bear the name of Christ, but few surrender their lives to Him. They miss the joy of the exchanged life: our weak, finite lives for His triumphant, eternal life — that is, His life in us as a true demonstration of His loving ways.

If both women and men would follow those ways, women would be the winners. We might as well admit it: we are physically weaker than men. That's why God tells men to protect and care for their wives: "Love your wives," He says, "just as Christ also loved the church and gave himself for her" (Eph. 5:25). That means putting her first, providing a safe place where she can be fulfilled. Believe it or not, innumerable men live out that command by God's grace.

Planned Deception

But God's ways have no place in the feminist agenda. Males have become enemies, not protectors, and it's time to even the score. Restoring harmony between the sexes, says Dr. Rosemary Ruether, "demands a rejection of all forms of patriarchal religions."[16] To win support for this cause, feminists must perpetuate the stereotypes of the violent, aggressive man and the passive, victimized woman.

The desperate strait of countless women around the world has been well-documented. Famine, war, social chaos, and dysfunctional families have put millions of women in physical and economic danger. Rape, torture, and murder have devastated war-torn nations. In the Sudan, girls are still circumcised as part of a coming-of-age ceremony. And the merchandising of women and girls in sweat factories and brothels amounts to a revival of slavery in some parts of the world.

Women *are* battered, abused, oppressed. They need help, loving support, and a shelter where they can feel safe. But you can't heal a culture by spreading hate. The early feminists won for us the right to vote. They opened doors to economic opportunities by using *old paradigm* tools such as fact, reason, and perseverance. But everything has changed. Facts gave way to propaganda, and truth to myths. And myths don't die as easily as they start.

Christina Hoff Sommers, who wrote *Who Stole Feminism,* has exposed some of these myths. She had read in *Revolution from Within* by Gloria Steinem that "in this country alone . . . about 150,000 females die of anorexia each year."[17] That seemed like a lot. More than three times the annual deaths from car accidents! So she traced the story back to its source. Ms. Steinem found her "facts" in Naomi Wolf's *The Beauty Myth*, which gave the same statistics but added an outrageous comparison between the Holocaust and "the emaciated bodies [of anorexia victims] starved not by nature but by men." *Starved by men?*

Miss Wolf got her figures from a former director of women's studies at Cornell University, who was "fully aware of the political significance of the startling statistics" and wanted to point out that "these disorders are an inevitable consequence of a misogynistic [hateful or distrustful] society that demeans women . . . by objectifying their bodies."[18] The Cornell professor attributed her figures to the American Anorexia and Bulimia Association (AABA).

"We were misquoted," said the president of the AABA when Ms. Sommers asked for the original data. Eventually, the true statistics came to light: the actual number of deaths from anorexia in 1991 were 54.[19] A far cry from 150,000! But the lie had already served its purpose: it validated feminist rage against male oppression and raised social consciousness everywhere.

"Why are certain feminists so eager to put men in a bad light?" asked Ms. Sommers. Ponder her conclusion:

> American feminism is currently dominated by a group of women who seek to persuade the public that American women are not the free creatures we think we are. . . . Believing that women are virtually under siege, the "gender feminists" naturally seek recruits to their side of the gender war. They seek support. They seek vindication. They seek ammunitions. . . . To confound the skeptics and persuade the unde-cided, the gender feminists are constantly on the lookout for the smoking gun, the telling fact that will drive home how profoundly the system is rigged against women . . . they must persuade us that the system itself sanctions male brutality.[20]

Militant Women

Hating men will only multiply our problems. Radical feminists know that — and cheer. They don't want to heal our nation. They want to tear it down. Every part of our "patriarchal" system must be dismantled — the family, the church, and our government — so they can recreate the world of their imagination. That means increasing the conflict and chaos — two vital ingredients to any effective revolution. They have come a long way, as you will see in chapter 9, which shows how the Beijing action plan hides global controls that are inconceivable to most Americans.

To understand the feminist revolution we need to

admit that men have no monopoly on violence. Women can be cruel and destructive, just as men can be gentle and compassionate. You may be surprised to hear that Hutu women joined in the savage butchering of at least half a million minority Tutsi adults and children in Rwanda a few years ago. After the slaughter, government officials admitted that "the role of women as killers and cheerleaders for murder was unprecedented in any other genocide this century."[21]

Please don't think I'm trying to demean women. I only want to expose the myths that block honest discussion and lasting solutions. The attitude that brings healing is not an arrogant and sexist "We're better than you." It is a willingness to confess our own vulnerability and say when someone fails, "But for God's grace, there go I."

"Females are at some periods just as intense, just as violent as the boys and in some cases more so," said Carl Taylor, a Michigan State University professor of family and child ecology.[22] His comment came after a local high school girl had attacked a classmate with a baseball bat. She faced charges of "assault with intent to murder." Concerning girls in general, the director of Detroit's Barat Human Services, Dianne Bostic Robinson, said, "We're finding them much more violent, not the nice little glove-wearing girls we saw years ago."[23]

Radical feminists are trying to shed that old image of girls. They don't want to be nice anymore. To them, strong men and amiable women symbolize the western culture they despise. Any form of authority other than their own is intolerable and must be crushed.

In *Sisterhood is Powerful*, Robin Morgan adds the nuclear family to the list of social villains. Quoting Frederick Engels, she says, "The modern individual family is founded on the open or concealed domestic slavery of the wife."[24] To Morgan, "the family is a decadent, energy-absorbing, destructive, wasteful institution for everyone except the ruling class, the class for which the institution was created."[25]

Those angry words are mobilizing the feminist army. By "helping" women see themselves as victims of male oppression, feminist leaders fuel the rage needed to achieve their revolution. By holding out promises like a carrot, they manipulate the anger according to their own agenda. But their lofty promises are just as hollow as their deceptive statistics. They promise great benefits, but they will eventually deliver the opposite:[26]

FEMINIST ACCUSATIONS AND VISIONS	
"Patriarchy" Caused	Feminism Promises
Powerlessness and self-condemnation	Empowerment and self-esteem
Harm and abuse	Renewal
Denial	Dignity and personhood
Dominance and inequality	Freedom and equality
Exclusion and injustice	Inclusion and justice
Hopelessness and depression	Joy and renewal
Dualism and separation	Unity and wholeness
Dominance	Equality
Limited to patriarchal spirituality	Blends all human experience

The feminist rage stirs a calculated kind of behavior. Studies show that when crowds are incited to action, individuals throw moral inhibitions and reason to the winds and yield their will to the group.[27] In other words, mass anger can easily become heartless and wild — just as it did among the murderous women in Rwanda.

While anger is a great motivator, it's a terrible healer. God has shown us a better way. By first defusing the rage, women could bring the pacifying touch of calm reason into the search for social healing. We should never tolerate injustice or close our eyes to pain. But for our own peace of mind, we can begin with a choice to forgive individuals who *actually* hurt us or others, then work together for answers without spreading venom of bitterness.

But women who have rejected the disciplines of truth find it hard to turn fury to forgiveness. Many choose a more natural response: swear, curse, scheme, shout . . . anything that placates the inner fire and feeds the fighting spirit.

Choosing to Curse

"People can choose to be open, loving, positive in each moment of their lives — or choose to be negative, resentful," Marianne Williamson told a reporter shortly after officiating at Liz Taylor's 1993 wedding. Bemused, her interviewer observed that the famed New Age author and counselor "seems to be choosing anger and resentment but [is] struggling to reign them in."[28]

At least Ms. Williamson tried. Others just give in to the rage. Some have even revived the ancient terrors of the curse. Strange as they may seem, curses accompany today's pagan revival. They often lead to their victims' death. At the Re-imagining Conference, Korean theologian Chung Hyun Kyung praised a Hindu ritual reminiscent of the emotional mob lynchings that cloud American history. Notice that feelings, not facts fed this ritual to the gruesome, bloodthirsty goddess Kali:

> I went to Sri Lanka . . . in front of Kali temple. . . . They have this ritual which is very simple and very striking. . . . [They] read all the names of the government officers [believed] to have killed their sons. . . . After calling all these men's names, she said only one thing: "Kali, let them be punished." Then 3,000 women brought one coconut apiece. In front of Kali they smashed coconuts on the ground . . . as an offering to Kali. But as outsider, I witnessed all these men's heads were

smashed when they smashed the coconuts, because Kali has all these necklaces [of skulls] and a beheaded man's skull in her hand. . . . *Kali is goddess of revenge and goddess of justice. . . .* She's fierce, she's uncontrollable . . . she's wild. Her power is not acceptable power but she uses this power to claim justice, to do justice.[29]

Kyung had begun her story by telling about her "new Trinity," the goddesses Kali, Kwan-in, and Enna, whom she discovered through her "participation in Asian women's movement." She closed by sharing her dream of "breaking coconuts in front of International Monetary Fund, the World Bank, the Vatican. . . ."

Her audience of 2,000 "Christian" women gave a hearty applause. Designing your own justice feels good to an untamed human nature.

All the more, this natural tendency to hurt rather than heal our "enemies" shows our desperate need for truth. "Vengeance *is* Mine," said God. "I will repay."[30] Only He has the wisdom to be fair. Our part is to love, however unnatural it may seem. But when we trust Him, He gives us what we need: tough, forgiving love — a love that "does not behave rudely, does not seek its own, is not provoked, thinks no evil; does not rejoice in iniquity, but rejoices in the truth; bears all things, believes all things, hopes all things, endures all things." (1 Cor. 13:6-7) This love seeks the kind of healing that can only be found in Jesus Christ who enables us:

- to understand the corruptive and contagious nature of sin;
- to build kind and caring communities;
- to humbly confess our sins to God and, when necessary, to each other;
- to let His forgiveness flow through us to others.

We can't do it ourselves, but He delights to do it in and through us!

Living in God's Forgiveness

Valerie learned it the hard way. She thought she had found the power to succeed, but the "Jesus" she met as a child turned out to be a counterfeit spirit who tormented her for 16 years — until she met the real Christ.

As far back as Valerie remembers, her family went to church. But at home, her television diet included "Bewitched," "Sabrina, the Teenage Witch," "Red Hot," and "Wendy, the Little Witch" — all shows that sugar-coated witchcraft and demonology. On Saturday mornings she watched captivating horror films. No one warned her about occult dangers. So when she was invited to play the Ouija board during a Halloween party at the home of a kindergarten classmate, she had no reason to refuse.

The instructions told them to start by inviting a spirit to come, so they prayed that the board would send someone. Then they put their fingertips on a smooth heart-shaped disc called a planchard and asked the spirit to tell its name. The planchard began to move. They stared amazed as it spelled SAINT PAUL. Could this be the Paul in the Bible? A real dead person? It answered YES. "How did you die?" asked Valerie. "CRUCIFIED," spelled the spirit. The children didn't catch the lie but, after a while, they did notice that it only answered Valerie's questions. "Why do you only answer Valerie?" asked one of the girls. This time it answered her — and spelled PSYCHIC.

Psychic? Valerie didn't know what the word meant, but it sounded important. She must be really special! Not only did she have special power from "Jesus," he sent her three invisible spirit friends named Patty, Jane, and Maureen. They sounded like teenage girls as they talked and argued inside her. "We were pals and hung out together," explained Valerie. "My parents thought they were just imaginary friends."

Prompted by her spirits, Valerie was always on the lookout for psychic literature. When Valerie's older sister bought the *Witches' Spell* and the *Encyclopedia on Witch-craft and Demonology* to fulfill a book club commitment, Valerie was the first to study them. No one connected the onset of her daily "petit mal seizures" with her occult interests.

By the time she was seven [yes, Valerie was a precocious learner], she was deeply engrossed in astrology, yet no one in her family seemed concerned. She knew that lying and stealing were wrong, but psychic things seemed innocent enough. After all, they seemed to work and didn't hurt anyone. They had to be from Jesus.

Each day, Valerie read her horoscope. The predictions were confusing sometimes, but when she looked hard enough for matching real-life experiences, she always found something. Later, with hindsight, she could see how those general predictions became self-fulfilling. Her attention was fixed on what she expected to see and her imagination was ready to comply.

Valerie's first grand mal seizure came during her first communion. She was sitting with her friends in the church, when she suddenly felt ill and stood up. Her body stiffened and shook with violent convulsions. It seemed as if something grabbed her, contorted her body, and threw her to the floor. Her startled friends thought she was dying. Dimly conscious, Valerie sensed that her hands clutched the air like claws and her gown was being pulled up over her head, making her feel violated and ashamed.

Strangely enough, her second "grand mal seizure" hit during her confirmation. Before she had time to confirm her faith in God, she lost consciousness. She remembered nothing afterwards, but the seizures became a regular part of her life. A doctor diagnosed and medicated her as an epileptic, but nothing stopped the convulsions.

Valerie was 14 when her mother died and her spirit guides convinced her to try suicide. "You'll go to heaven anyway," they coached. "You're a good kid." A miraculous intervention hindered her death, but life became increasingly painful. Sometimes she found herself speaking in "counterfeit tongues" — or barking, growling, and saying nonsense words that shocked her peers. A series of physical and sexual attacks increased her fear and isolation. Alone, she would console herself with her three spirit pals who were training her for the craft.

In college, Valerie became a "white witch" and learned to "cast circles in Jesus' name." Her spirit guides told her to marry Keith, a warlock obsessed by the occult role-playing game "Dungeons and Dragons." Trained to do their will, she agreed and was soon engaged. Her obedience was rewarded with a well-paying job as a fortune teller. "I still thought I was doing God's will," said Valerie years later. "I called myself 'a witch for Jesus.' "

In spite of all the medical tests and prescriptions, the daily seizures grew worse. One day a theology student named Martin happened to see her convulse. When it ended, he helped her back on her feet and took her home. Inside her apartment, he noticed her shelves full of Wiccan manuals, crystals, amulets, and other occult paraphernalia.

Frightened, he said, "Valerie, this is a bad thing you're doing."

"No, it's not," she answered. "What do you know about this? You're into your craft for the Lord, and I'm doing mine."

"I'm going to pray for you," he replied.

"Okay, pray for me. It won't hurt."

From then on, Martin often helped her through the seizures. "Valerie," he said one day, "come with me to my church."

She agreed. The next Sunday, sitting in a pew, an awareness of God's holiness swept through her. Suddenly, she saw — as if through His eyes — the evil she had embraced. "I felt so filthy and ashamed," she explained later. "I just wanted to cover myself up. It was as if God told me, 'Change now, or you'll never be safe. Your heart will become so hardened you will never be able to hear Me.' I asked God to forgive me for all the awful things I had done, and I knew He did. I knelt on the floor and sobbed with joy. The change was incredible. I felt so different, so clean inside."

Back at her apartment, Valerie knew what to do. "I've got to get rid of some stuff," she told Martin. She threw everything — books, crystals, amulets, ritual music, even the rock and roll stuff — into a big lawn bag. She wanted a brand new start, and thanked God that she had already broken her engagement to Keith.

Two years later Valerie married Martin. They moved and found a Bible-teaching church. Finally, Valerie began to learn the truths about the God she had mistakenly assumed she knew all her life. Visiting her pastor one day, she told him about her own dark journey.

"Did you ever go through deliverance?" he asked her.

"No," she answered. "What is that?"

He explained that she needed to renounce every occult practice she had embraced and be freed from all demonic connections. She was more than willing, so they agreed to do it on the spot. In prayer, Valerie disclaimed everything she could remember: the Ouija board, astrology, spiritism, divination, necromancy (communicating with supposed spirits of the dead), channeling, the tarot cards, and spell working — the "abominations" mentioned in Deuteronomy 18:9-12. She trusted God to break every link to occult forces.

The spirits resisted. Valerie's chair began to sway and horrible demonic voices began to speak. "We're not leaving," they mocked. "You have no power." But the pastor called their bluff and, with the authority of Christ who commissioned him, he commanded them to get out. They had to obey and Valerie was finally free. What Jesus did for the child in Luke 9:42, He had done for her: "The demon threw him to the ground in a convulsion. But Jesus rebuked the evil spirit [and] healed the boy."

Before the session ended, Valerie confessed her own readiness to welcome spirit guides, her Wiccan profession, and her part in leading others into darkness. One by one, the Holy Spirit brought the memories to the surface of her mind so she could take every sin to the Cross and receive the pardon and cleansing Jesus had bought with His own life. "Thank You, my Lord," she whispered as the words of her favorite psalm began to flow through her mind:

> Have mercy upon me, O God,
> According to Your lovingkindness. . . .
> Wash me thoroughly from my iniquity,
> And cleanse me from my sin. . . .
> Create in me a clean heart, O God,
> And renew a steadfast spirit within me. . . .
> Restore to me the joy of Your salvation,
> And uphold me *by Your* generous Spirit. . . .
> (Ps. 51:1-17)

God answered her prayer — and gave far more than she asked. Not only did the *real* Jesus fill her with His life and love, Valerie never had another seizure, nor did she face the usual withdrawal symptoms when she stopped the medication.

Filled with the Holy Spirit, she was able to forgive all who had hurt and abused her. One by one, she extended His forgiving love to them — to some only in the secret of His presence, to others by mail. For how could she — who had been forgiven so much — refuse the same kind of forgiveness to others?

Often, since then, the beautiful promise of Luke 7:47-49 has come to mind: "Therefore I say to you, her sins, which are many, are forgiven, for she loved much. But to whom little is forgiven, the same loves little. . . . Your faith has saved you. Go in peace." Jesus, who is *the* Truth, had indeed set her free.[31]

Freedom is the heart-cry of feminism — freedom *from* authority, injustice, moral boundaries — and freedom *to* chart your own way. The next chapter will show why no freedom can be found in the feminist movement.

Endnotes

[1] Marianne Williamson, A Return to Love (New York, NY: Harper Collins, 1992), p. 138.

[2] Manuela Dunn Mascetti, *The Song of Eve* (New York, NY: Simon & Schuster, 1990), p. 86.

[3] *The Whole People of God* (Grove Heights, MN: Logos Productions, 1993), p. 15.

[4] Ibid., p. 16.

[5] Galatians 5:19-21.

[6] Lois Wilson, Re-imagining Conference, November 6, 1993. Tape 7-1, Side B.

[7] Kathy Kersten, "Looking for God in the Mirror," *Bibliscope* (May-June, 1994), p. 2.

[8] Kimberley Snow, *Keys to the Open Gate* (Berkeley, CA: Conari Press, 1994), 263.

[9] Patricia Eagle, *Book of Shadows*. Cited by Snow, *Keys to the Open Gate*, p. 76.

[10] Susan Cyre, "College Women's Packet Promotes Goddess Worship," *The Presbyterian Layman*, May/June 1993.

[11] Ibid. The Evangelism and Church Development Ministry Unit of the Presbyterian Church USA gave $85,000 to the Women's Ministry Unit to underwrite a project called "Witness to Women" believing it would be used "to reach unchurched." The Coordinating Committee of the College Women's Network developed materials using classic feminist strategies designed to disciple new converts to feminism rather than to Jesus Christ.

[12] Marianne Williamson, *A Woman's Worth* (New York, NY: Ballantine Books, 1993), p. 15-16.

[13] Ibid., p. 17.

[14] Robert Jewett, "Response to the service honoring Sophia," May 9, 1995. Dr. Jewett cited *Anchor Bible Dictionary* I.226.

[15] "Goddess litany at UM seminary chapel ignites controversy," *Good News* (September/October 1995); 35.

[16] Transcribed from taped address by Rosemary Radford Ruether on "Healing Violence to Creation" at the Renaissance of Christian Spirituality Conference presented by the California Institute of

Integral Studies, March 25, 1995. Transcribed from tape #2.

[17]Christina Hoff Sommers, "Figuring Out Feminism, *National Review* (June 27, 1994), p. 30.

[18]Ibid. Referring to (not quoting) Joan Brumberg who wrote *Fasting Girls: The Emergence of Anorexia Nervosa as a Modern Disease.*

[19]Reported by Thomas Dunn of the Division of Vital Statistics at the National Center for Health Statistics. Cited by Christina Hoff Sommers.

[20]Christina Hoff Sommers, "Figuring Out Feminism," *National Review* (June 27, 1994) p. 32.

[21]Patrick McDowell, "Women's Role in Rwanda Genocide," *San Francisco Chronicle*, September 26, 1995.

[22]Associated Press, *The Oakland Press*, March 13, 1994.

[23]Ibid.

[24]Frederick Engels, *Origin of the Family, Private Property, and the State.* Cited by Robin Morgan, Ed., *Sisterhood is Powerful:* An Athology of Writings from the women's Liberation Movement (New York: Vintage Books, 1970), p. 546.

[25]Robin Morgan, Ed., *Sisterhood is Powerful:* An Athology of Writings from the Women's Liberation Movement (New York, NY: Vintage Books, 1970), p. 546.

[26]Chapters 8, 9, and 10 will explain why.

[27]Gustave Le Bon wrote in *The Crowd* (Burlington, VT: Fraser Publishing Co., 1982), xvi, xx, 9: "Little adapted to reasoning, crowds are quick to act. . . . How powerless they are to hold any opinions other than those which are *imposed upon them.* . . . [They are led] by seeking what produces an impression on them and what seduces them." Crowds possess a "collective mind which makes them feel, think and act in a manner quite different. . . . [The member of a crowd gains] a sentiment of invincible power which allows [him] to yield to instincts which, had he been alone, he would . . . have kept under restraint.

[28]Mike Capuzzo, "The Divine Ms. W," *The Sacramento Bee*, May 30, 1993.

[29]Re-Imagining Conference Tape 2-2, Side A.

[30]Romans 12:19.

[31]John 8:32, 36.

Chapter 7

Lead Us Not into Temptation Versus Temptation? I Create My Own Values

～

We are not just passing on our theologies. . . . We are responsible for shaping them in new times. (Mary Farrell Bednarowski, speaker, Re-imagining Conference)[1]

Every woman has the birthright to . . . strip culturally imposed roles and unveil her own mystery. (Deborah Turner-Bey)[2]

We listen to our bodies, minds and emotions to inform us about truth — our own and others. . . . We draw forth our creativity and self-expression as images for what is welling up in us. (Women's Alliance)[3]

No temptation has overtaken you except such as is common to man; but God is faithful, who will not allow you to be tempted beyond what you are able, but with the temptation will also make the

way of escape, that you may be able to bear it. (1
Cor. 10:13)

⌒⌒⌒

Graceful like a dancer, Christina moved across the
stage. Above her hung the flags of the nations and a banner
announcing "The State of the World" — a five-day global
conference convened in San Francisco by Mikhail
Gorbachev.[4] The theme and its vision of global renewal fit
her well, for in her flowing white maternity gown and long
golden hair, she resembled a New Age painting of an
ethereal earth goddess ready to birth new life. Clutching the
microphone, she began to sing a prayer to her universal god:

> O faithful One . . . I call on thee
> O holy one, O helping one. . . .
> Abiding hope, I call on thee
> Beloved, compassionate, source of all being
> O God of grace, come down.

The prayer, she explained, was from her Baha'i prayer
book. The music was her own, supposedly given by the
unknowable, compassionate god of Hinduism, of Buddhism, of Christianity, and of all spiritual avatars throughout time.

Christina's global spirituality set the stage for the
evening plenary — a metaphysical message by top-selling
author Dr. Deepak Chopra, director of the Institute for
Mind/Body Medicine in San Diego. "The universe is seeking to fulfill itself through us," he said. "Are we up to the
responsibility?" His next point shows the much-repeated
motif of the conference:

> Can you step out of the river of your own
> conditioning and see the world as if for the first
> time? For only then is there an opportunity to
> create a new body — but more importantly, a *new
> world*. We cannot do it the way we have done it in

the past. *It is time to change the whole paradigm through which we view physical reality.*

The political, spiritual, and business leaders gathered in San Francisco on the evening of September 28, 1995, had already made that paradigm shift. By the third day, it was obvious to me that the speakers and their enthusiastic audience, including Barbara Marx Hubbard and Jane Fonda, saw reality from a decidedly global perspective. Again and again, Gorbachev and his hand-picked "global brain trust" told over 1,000 guests and participants that new universal values were needed to guide the world into the 21st Century. These values must replace the Christian world view, eradicate poverty and oppression, and establish a new kind of tolerance, unity, and equality.

That their noble goals clashed with more selfish interests didn't bother the world's leading visionaries. One moment they decried human injustice; the next, they bemoaned human existence. "Don't feed them," suggested Ted Turner in a discussion on reducing consumption to save the earth. Sam Keen, author of best-seller *Fire in the Belly,* made an even more provocative statement in his summary of the discussions on the Global Crisis of Spirit and the Search for Meaning:

> Religious institutions . . . must speak far more clearly about sexuality, about contraception, about abortion, about values that control the population, because the ecological crisis, in short, *is* the population crisis. *Cut the population by 90 percent and there aren't enough people left to do a great deal of ecological damage.*

At the end of the conference, the publisher of *Earth Vision* magazine told me about her disappointment over the seeming hypocrisy. "I don't believe they really care all that much about the poor," she said. "An evening meal here costs over $120 per person, yet they talk about equality, justice, and raising consciousness. Why couldn't they have served just one meal of rice? That would have done more to raise our awareness than all their promising words."

Just then, Shirley McLaine walked by, so I asked her what she thought of the conference.

"It was good. It helped raise consciousness," she answered.

"But wouldn't it have raised consciousness more if one of the meals had just been rice instead of gourmet meat and elegant desserts?"

She frowned. "People paid a lot of money to come here," she answered. "They deserved good food."

What Do Women Really Want?

The new paradigm is here, and its noble visions hide all kinds of ignoble plans. We may all agree on a few "universal values" such as love, peace, and unity. But who has to conform in order to create the new unity — feminists or traditional women? Even when we agree on the words, we may disagree on the meanings. You've seen how values differ from one paradigm to the other, and the loftiest of them may fade in the light of earthier wants such as dessert, clothes, power, and popularity.

It's easy to hide personal wants behind utopian visions and global spirituality. That's what Gorbachev's global conference did. Psychotherapist Deena Metzger did the same in her article, "Re-Vamping the World: On the Return of the Holy Prostitute:"

> Once upon a time, in Sumeria, in Mesopotamia, in Egypt, in Greece, there were no whorehouses, no brothels. . . . There were instead the Temples of the Sacred Prostitutes. In these temples, men were cleansed, not sullied, morality was restored, not desecrated, sexuality was not perverted, but divine.
>
> The original whore was a priestess, the con-

duit to the Divine, the one through whose body one entered the sacred arena and was restored. . . .

It is no wonder that . . . the prophets of Jehovah all condemned the Holy Prostitute and the worship of Asherah, Astarte, Anath, and the other goddesses. Until the time of these priests the women were the one doorway to God.[5]

Do you see the two paradigms? One sees reality through the filter of biblical truth; the other looks through the lens of feeling-based paganism. From Ms. Metzger's new-paradigm perspective, the sex rites of ancient Middle Eastern paganism sound great. To the Old Testament prophets, they looked bad. Ms. Metzger needed a story that would tell her side, so she used her imagination. It filtered out facts that clashed with her vision and embellished those that fit. She understood the process well: "Whatever rites we imagine took place . . . [depends on] whether we elevate them as do neo-pagans or condemn them as do Judeo-Christians." Today, some link the ancient prostitutes to "orgies and debauchery." Others link them to cleansing and divinity. Most choose something in between.

Some of Ms. Metzger's feminist sisters would probably disagree that the ancient practice of "sacred" and compulsory prostitution is good for the soul, but that doesn't matter. Women don't have to agree. Today, each woman may claim the right to stand unchallenged on her own truth and values, and Metzger's "truth" sounds good to those who prefer to cloak sex with spirituality.

Janie Spahr, co-founder of CLOUT (Christian Lesbians Out Together), links sex to sacredness. "Sexuality and spirituality have come together, and Church, we're going to teach you!" she announced at the Re-imagining Conference.[6] Her theology, she explained, is first of all informed by "making love with Coni," her lesbian lover. Is she implying, as modern pagans do, that sex is a channel for spiritual energy?

"Sexuality is a sacrament," writes Starhawk, the Wiccan

author you met in chapter 4. "Religion is a matter of relinking, with the divine within and with her outer manifestation in all of the human and natural world."[7]

"In a sacred universe," continued Ms. Metzger, "the prostitute is a holy woman, a priestess. In a secular universe, the prostitute is a whore. . . . The question is: how do we relate to this today, as women, as feminists? Is there a way we can resanctify society, become the priestesses again, put ourselves in the service of the gods and Eros? As we re-vision, can we re-vamp as well?"[8]

The answer is a resounding "yes." People have already re-visioned sex. The "vamping" process is well underway. Just look at television and newspaper ads. Our Sunday morning papers as well as contemporary women's magazines parade the same titillating pictures once hidden in private pin-up calendars. Our culture has been cut loose from its moorings, and any new current can take it for a ride. That the feminist movement flows in the same direction as Gorbachev's — at least for the moment — only speeds it forward.

Yet, like the proverbial frog in the slow-heating water, most people haven't noticed.

Freely Female

Dancing bare-breasted to music from a make-shift stage in a Michigan forest, a woman spun, swayed, and rejoiced, while her more inhibited new friends watched with admiration. Joining nearly 8,000 other women, she had come to the annual Womyn's Music Festival seeking "wisdom in a society where the only rules, the only standards of beauty and femininity, are their own."[9]

Calling themselves "womyn" to distance themselves from men, they had come from "as far away as Australia," wrote reporter Robin Givhan. For six days they would empower themselves through aboriginal music, Native American rituals, and unforgettable workshops on such topics as feminism and women's cycles. Serving no god but themselves, they could worship their bodies and honor their own blood. There's no need for the cleansing blood of Christ.

A matriarchal leader who called herself Coyote lead a workshop called "Our Sacred Bloods: An introduction to Women's Mysteries." Nude, except for a sarong around her waist, she clasped the hands of the women at her sides and formed a ritual circle to draw power from the earth. Together they would "tap into the energy created by thousands of women working together in their utopia."[10]

Utopias are deceptive illusions, yet utopian beliefs can be far more resistant to reason than stark reality. When these beliefs match politically correct thinking as well as the cravings of human nature, the facts make little difference. Remember, Satan usually tempts us with lures that match our basic desires. If it feels good, looks good, and sounds good, we want it. Even God's most noble values — love, peace, and unity — can be twisted into lies that serve a contrary purpose.

All values sprout from basic beliefs or assumptions. The values that first molded our nation were based on biblical truth — not Iroquois government as some historical revisionists claim.[11] The new values are rooted in these New Age and neo-pagan assumptions:

- The earth and all its parts are sacred.
- Therefore everything is naturally good.
- Therefore I am sacred and good.
- Therefore there is no sin.
- Everything is connected to the same spiritual source.
- Therefore insights from my "inner self" are true.
- Therefore you and I can find "common ground."
- Therefore biblical Christianity doesn't fit.

God shows us the opposite way: love Him first, share His love with others, then we discover our identity in Him. As you can see, the two ways are incompatible:

OPPOSING VALUES	
Biblical Christian	**Feminist Neo-pagan**
Knowing God	Knowing divine self
Finding God's will	Getting in touch with one's feelings
Loving God, then each other	Loving self, then others
Oneness with God and other Christians	Unity with everything
Loving sinners, hating sin	Tolerance for anything (except *in*tolerance)

Look at the following from a new paradigm perspective. See the difference:

• Unity means compromise — according to new paradigm rules. A Christian's refusal to compromise her beliefs is unacceptable.

• Freedom means *my* right to express myself without hindrance from family or culture. It doesn't include another woman's right to express herself, if her words or action threaten my comfort zone.

• Peace means agreeing to tolerate all beliefs and people — except Christianity and those who refuse to respect my lifestyle.

The key to the feminist transformation is *tolerance* — tolerance for all the new feminist values, ways, and lifestyles. This politically correct tolerance, which shows no tolerance toward the old ways and values, is essential to silencing all critics.

Unholy Tolerance

Life has changed at St. Olaf College since I was a

student there. Years ago, Minnesota's venerable "college on the hill" seemed the ultimate in both Christian and Lutheran education. But multi-cultural education has replaced biblical integrity, and a new global emphasis has opened the door to professors who promote Hindu and other "mind-body" beliefs instead of biblical truth.[10] The chapel, once a sacred sanctuary for worshiping God, has become a moral battleground.

One spring morning in 1989, English teacher Rebecca Mark gave the chapel talk. She first introduced the point of her message:

> To speak the words, "I am gay. I am proud to be gay," at this place where silence has reigned too long, is not enough. I am not alone. . . . I am called upon to be the voice of many who have been silent. . . .
>
> As a gay woman I speak through the earth. The word gay comes from the goddess Gaia, the Greek earth mother goddess. I speak not as a sinner, but as the Mojave shaman. . . . I speak from the voice of thousands of gay spirit leaders, healers, and teachers in Indian culture. . . . I speak as . . . those who have known death and rebirth. And I, too, mourn. . . .

Ms. Mark mourned the cruel slurs and spiteful rejection suffered by gay students, and she was right to do so. God calls us to love, not hate those who miss the mark. His love reaches out to all who hurt, including those who yield their bodies to promiscuous lifestyles, whether homosexual or heterosexual. But Mark's call reached far beyond a condemnation of cruelty. It sent a vision of multi-cultural solidarity that demands a radical change in the very heart of Christianity. It summoned God's people to not only approve promiscuous and destructive lifestyles,[13] but also embrace the pagan spirituality that sacrilizes sex.

She ended her talk with a sensual poem by an American Indian woman who blended lesbian love with a spiritualized earth mother. Then she invited the students and faculty — all who "can wear the pink triangle proudly" — to come forward as a "sign of community and liberation." Singing "We are gay and straight together," they streamed to the front of the church to claim the badge of their new identity.

The enthusiastic response was no surprise, for our today's culture prefers tolerance to truth. So did ancient Israel. "Why do you tolerate wrong?"[14] God asked the people He loved, knowing that their presumptuous tolerance would lead to violence and destruction. They didn't listen. Neither does our culture today. (Look up tolerance in your Bible concordance and see what God says about it.) Instead, we excuse what He calls sin and mock the peace He longs to give. The results are devastating.

Read what He says about sex outside marriage.

> Flee sexual immorality. Every sin that a man does is outside the body, but he who commits sexual immorality sins against his own body. Or do you not know that your body is the temple of the Holy Spirit *who is* in you, whom you have from God, and you are not your own? For you were bought at a price; therefore glorify God in your body and in your spirit, which are God's (1 Cor. 6:18-20).

The Nature of Temptation

God shows us that sexual sins are especially damaging to us both physically and spiritually. Yet, neo-pagans tout the healing and cleansing effects of "sacred" promiscuity. Interesting twist, isn't it?

Those who tolerate sin become blind to its meaning. Women cannot maintain utopian illusion unless they hide opposing truths. They can't trust their sacred self without rationalizing away its unholy bent. So they shift God's label for sin away from the things they want and attach it to things they despise: Promiscuity? That comes from loss of self-esteem caused by the guilt feelings stirred up by Christians who criticize my lifestyle. Anger? Try the same reasoning.

Do you see how easy it is to be "good" if you use the "right" reasoning? Just re-imagine the old values. Base your beliefs on your momentary feelings, not on God's time-tested Word. Look at the difference a paradigm shift makes.

SIN IS. . . .	
Biblical Paradigm	**Feminist Paradigm**
separation from God	separation from (spiritual forces in) nature
rebelling against God	ignoring the god(dess) in self
self-centeredness	not loving self first
pride	lack of pride
lack of self-discipline	limiting self-fulfillment
disobeying God	submitting to a patriarchal god
tolerating sin	not tolerating sin

Tolerating sin destroys shame. Some years ago, I watched the pastor's wife in a Presbyterian (USA) church teach a Sunday school class called "Women at the Well." She first "centered" the class with a chant by medieval mystic Hildegaard of Bingen whose pantheistic images sounded more Buddhist than Christian. Then she read a quote by Thomas Merton, the Catholic mystic who embraced Tibetan Buddhism. Finally she gave us a two-page handout from a book called *Soul Friend: An Invitation to Spiritual Direction.*[15] It told me that today's mysticism, which blends acceptance of sin with a permissive feminine God, isn't all that new:

> In the fourteenth century in Europe there was a great flowering of **mysticism**, and out of this period came some of the greatest spiritual guides of all time whose writings are highly relevant today. . . .
>
> Julian of Norwich . . . claims that "God showed me that sin need be no shame to man but can even be worthwhile." She seems to mean by this that sins are disguised virtues, for "in heaven what sin typifies is turned into a thing of honour."[16]
>
> In Julian's theology, we find the fullest expression of the concept of the femininity of God. "God is as really our Mother as he is Father," she says. "Our precious Mother Jesus brings us to supernatural birth, nourishes and cherishes us by dying for us."[17]

It's true that our sins show us our need for Christ's redemption, but they are *not* "disguised virtues." They don't typify something of honor, nor can they be softened by putting a feminine face on God. We can live without shame only because God has forgiven us, not because sin has lost its sting. If I condone my own sins, I will neither come to the Cross nor appreciate God's wonderful mercy. Nor would I fight the seductive pull of Satan's temptations — especially those that look almost too good to resist.

As you saw in chapter 6, Satan can only pervert God's good. Our Father invented delightful food, human affection, sexual pleasure, satisfying work, spiritual insights. Everything good came from Him. Satan can only distort and imitate God's precious gifts, or tempt us to grasp too much or too little, or take it at the wrong time, or in the wrong place. You know the results: pain, confusion, anger, addiction, broken relationships, decaying culture, and much more. (See the rest in Gal. 5:19-25.)

Temptations can be aimed at our body, soul, or spirit, and Satan knows which part of us is most vulnerable at any time. He tries to incite the *body* to crave physical sensation, the *soul* to desire emotional stimulation, and the human *spirit* to seek supernatural experience, "higher" wisdom, affirmations, etc.—often in territories outside those made safe by God. Like foolish sheep who leave the green fields of the shepherd for an illusion of richer fields behind the fence, we follow Eve's example:

> So when the woman saw that the tree *was* good for food *[body]*, that it was pleasant to the eyes *[soul]*, and desirable to make one wise *[spirit]*, she took of its fruit and ate (Gen. 3:6).

> For all that is in the world — the lust of the flesh *[body]*, the lust of the eyes *[soul]*, and the pride of life *[spirit]* — is not of the Father but is of the world (1 John 2:16).

The things God labels as sinful lust, the world now sees as psychological addiction or obsession for which a person is not responsible.[18] Denying sin's power doesn't soften its consequences. "Each one is tempted when he is drawn away by his own desires and enticed. Then, when desire has conceived, it gives birth to sin; and sin, when it is full-grown, brings forth death" (James 1:14-15).

Utopian Dreams Lead Where?

"If we make a god of sexuality, that god will fail in ways that affect the whole person and perhaps the whole society," wrote author Philip Yancey.[19] One day while browsing through a university library, he discovered a 1934 book called *Sex and Culture* by scholar J. D. Unwin. It showed Yancey a direct tie between monogamy and the "expansive energy" of civilization. Unwin, who had studied the sexual practices of 86 different cultures, concluded that:

In human records there is no instance of a society retaining its energy after a complete new generation has inherited a tradition which does not insist on pre-nuptial and post-nuptial continence.[20]

Did you hear that? Sexual immorality led to social decay. Babylon, Sumeria, Greece, Rome, and other ancient pagan civilizations disintegrated when sexual boundaries disappeared. While temple prostitution and ritual sex had been permitted within prescribed boundaries from the beginning, unbridled promiscuity had been taboo. Its return signaled cultural decline.

Unwin couldn't explain why. But the pattern he saw impressed him enough to propose that British citizens "take vows of chastity before marriage and observe strict monogamy after marriage — all for the sake of the Empire."

God's principles can bring order into chaos even when followed by non-Christians. For those who trust God, they bring triumph. But those who reject them suffer consequences they can't understand. Yancey showed why:

For the Christian, sex is not an end in itself but, rather, a gift from God. Like all such gifts, it must be stewarded according to God's rules, not ours.[19]

That our schools have taught the opposite for decades, has caused untold damage to our youth and culture. Listen to the philosophy behind the sex education promoted by SIECUS (Sex Information and Education Council of the United States):

The purpose of sex education is not . . . to control and suppress sex expression, as in the past. . . . The individual must be given sufficient understanding to *incorporate sex most fruitfully and most responsibly into his present and future life*. (Emphasis added)[21]

SIECUS has been working with Planned Parenthood to bring social change. The behavior inspired by their irresponsible agenda has brought devastating results. Consider these statistics:

> • Every 24 hours in this nation more than 12,000 teenagers contract a sexually transmitted disease. Thirty percent of all STD's contracted are incurable.[23]
> • Each year 1.3 million new cases of gonorrhea are reported.[24]
> • One million teenage girls, nearly one in 10, become pregnant each year.[25]
> • About 1.5 million unborn babies are aborted each year.

"Current sex education programs are designed to destroy the normal embarrassment and modesty of children," writes Stanley Monteith, M.D., author of *AIDS: The Uneccessary Epidemic,* in his informative newsletter, "yet it is that modesty that has traditionally been a barrier to early sexual experimentation and promiscuity."[26]

The root problems aren't homosexuality or promiscuity or even paganism. It is the loss of truth as our moral standard. When school teachers blur the line between right and wrong, why should students say "no" to temptation? Why not try all the "new" sensations that beckon? Young people do — and face cravings they can't control. Unlike biblical love, lust will not wait; and obsessive lust has a way of displacing God's kind and patient love.

Bondage can follow any repeated sin. "Therefore do not let sin reign in your mortal body, that you should obey it in its lusts," warns Paul.[27] But many feminists who claim control over their bodies have already yielded that control to a stronger force. Most women "make a choice for life when they take up smoking as teen-agers," concluded a study by the Centers for Disease Control and Prevention. "Three quarters of them will find it too difficult to quit later."[28]

"Most of the things likely to produce enduring happiness — education, employment, stable families — require us to forego immediate pleasures," writes Columnist George Will. "What happens when that discipline fails? Look around."[29]

It doesn't take long to see results. We have become a society obsessed with sex, food, looks, shopping, drugs, gambling, and coddling our feelings. But we feel no shame, because we dare not name sin. As a schoolgirl said when her 15-year-old classmate stabbed another student in the back. "What's the big deal? People die all the time. So what?"[30]

From Tolerance to Disillusionment

Any sin is a big deal. Even the smallest ones will separate us from God if we don't follow His way back to peace. Neo-pagans may deny sin's power, Buddhists may offer noble alternatives, and the New Age movement may inspire a massive leap in consciousness, but they all miss the point. Humanity can never evolve beyond its need for the Cross.

Some years ago the Dalai Lama, god-king of Tibetan Buddhists, stopped by the Bay Area to teach "empowerment" rituals at San Jose State University and to "invoke the spirits of this area" on Mount Tamalpais. After summoning "the blessings of enlightened spiritual masters" such as the Lord Buddha, Jesus Christ, and Mohammed in a healing and peace ceremony, he would lead San Francisco's religious leaders in a joint commitment to pursue world peace.

The newspaper made occult healing sound so normal. Saddened by the promotion of spiritism, I prayed that God would block the demonic forces. The morning of the scheduled appearance I drove to Grace Cathedral and once again joined the waiting throng, knowing that friends at home prayed with me for God's intervention.

The Dalai Lama was scheduled to arrive at 3 p.m. On the hour, heads turned back toward the huge doors. At 3:20

we were still waiting. And at 3:45, creaking benches and impatient voices suggested that people were growing weary of waiting. Finally, an hour late, the doors swung open. Enveloped in a smoky cloud of incense — believed to purify the environment and heal relationships — the procession of spiritual leaders marched up the aisle. All except the Dalai Lama. Our eyes stayed fixed on the back doors.

"Unfortunately the Dalai Lama is indisposed," said a voice from the podium. The unwelcome words crushed all hope. In the midst of confused whispers and a few hurried departures, the ceremony proceeded with prayers from various church leaders. But the sound system didn't work. "We can't hear!" shouted the people. But nobody solved the problem.

Walking out after the aborted ceremony, I noticed a woman crying. "Are you all right?" I asked. She didn't answer. "Would you like to talk or would you rather be alone?" I didn't want to intrude.

"I'm so disappointed," she burst out. "This was such a failure. I couldn't even hear what they said."

"It was confusing, wasn't it? How could the Dalai Lama be disabled after the healing ceremony this morning?"

Sadness filled Sue's voice as she answered. "I don't understand. It sounded so perfect. All the religions joining together. Why did everything go wrong?"

Seeking answers that would touch her heart, I prayed. Suddenly thoughts began to flow. I said, "Maybe God doesn't like our attempts to control the world and seek oneness apart from Him."

"Why wouldn't He want us to get together and make the world more peaceful?"

"Maybe He knows that our plans wouldn't work, and that by trusting ourselves and magic powers rather than Him, we would lose sight of the only real hope we have."

"But the Dalai Lama trusts God. His monks just came from the Vatican where they talked with the Pope and his monks about unity and meditation."

"I wonder what kind of unity Christians can enjoy with Buddhist monks without compromising their faith. Christianity is God-centered and Buddhism is self-centered." I waited a moment before continuing. "I don't dare rely on myself anymore. It's so much easier to admit my weaknesses and trust the only One who can give me the strength I need — Jesus Christ."

"But why is He any better than the other great teachers? They all taught the same things. They all said we should love each other and be kind and tolerant."

"Many did say that. I guess everyone knows deep inside that love is good and hate is bad. It seems to be part of the understanding God puts in each of us. But none of those religions can do more than *tell* us what to do. Then each person has to muster the strength to follow their ideals on their own in the midst of all kinds of problems and irritations. I don't think I could do that."

"Isn't that why we need to learn tolerance? We have to love and tolerate each other so we can live in peace."

"But the Christian God does more than that. He wants to fill us with His life and peace so we can do what is right. He knows we can't do it ourselves, so He enables us."

We talked a long time. Her futile search for peace had led her on and off numerous spiritual paths. Now, in her frustration, she was ready to listen to the only One who could love, shepherd, and fulfill her. We prayed together and agreed to meet again soon.

All the way home I praised my Lord, who once again had proven himself the sovereign, omnipotent King of kings.

Dealing with Temptation

Sue began her search when disillusioned with "Christians" in the church she was raised. Her disappointment begs the question: If Christ is King and He lives in us, why don't we *always* demonstrate His love? I can think of several reasons. One is simply that we focus on the wrong values. We let the tempter turn us away from what God wants for us to seductive substitutes. Though we want to do "our utmost for His highest,"[31] we choose to live by more earthy values. To escape the trap, look how Jesus dealt with temptation.

Jesus felt painfully weak after 40 days without food. Satan knew it, so he suggested that Jesus use His divine power to turn a stone into bread — an easy miracle for the King of the universe. But Jesus had already made up His mind *not* to use supernatural strength to escape His own suffering. So He countered the temptation with a Bible verse that pointed to a higher value. "It is written," He said, claiming the authority of Scriptures, " 'Man shall not live by bread alone, but by every word of God.' "[32]

Ready with more tricks, the devil showed Him the riches of the world and offered to give it all to Jesus if He would fall down and worship him. Weak as He was, Jesus again looked from a temporal value to an eternal good: "You shall worship the Lord your God, and Him only you shall serve."

Finally, the devil brought Him to the pinnacle of the temple, and suggested that Jesus demonstrate His godly authority. Determined not to deviate from His plan, Jesus answered, "It has been said, 'You shall not tempt the Lord your God.' "

The devil finally gave up and left Jesus alone "until an opportune time" (Luke 4:13).

Food, riches, and power all have value, but God's Word is worth far more. Miracles and great testimonies can strengthen our faith, but they can also bring pride along with praise and may actually weaken our trust in what God does through "ordinary" circumstances.

The key to victory is hidden in the words of an old hymn:

> Turn your eyes upon Jesus
> Look full in His wonderful face;

> And the things of earth will grow strangely dim
> In the light of His glory and grace.

When we focus on God's highest and best, we won't settle for second best. As long as we see reality — human needs, suffering, injustice — from a human perspective, we'll pick the wrong solutions. But when we ask God to show us life from His heavenly perspective, everything looks different. All the hurts and irritations fade in the light of who God really is, and in the wonder of His eternal plan.

God rarely picks the easiest course for us, for His training process is far more important than our shortsighted goals. If we want power to please ourselves, He may use tedious chores to train us to take our self-focused goals to the cross. If we want to fulfill lofty humanitarian visions, He may first teach us to prove His love among unloving people. His way up may first lead down — down to the place where we best learn the lesson of trusting God no matter where He leads us. Jesus, not only tells us so; He walked there first:

> Let this mind be in you which was also in Christ Jesus, who, being in the form of God . . . made himself of no reputation, taking the form of a bondservant, *and* coming in the likeness of men. And being found in appearance as a man, He humbled himself and became obedient to *the point of* death, even the death of the cross (Phil. 2:5-8).

On that Cross, we were saved — we were "crucified with Christ,"[33] freed from the *power* of sin. If we are joined to Him by faith, we can now choose to let His love rule our lives — or to do our own thing. If we choose His way, our human weakness becomes an opportunity to demonstrate His strength. For "God has chosen the weak things of the world to put to shame the things which are mighty" (Cor. 1:27).

Admitting our sin to God softens the human tendency

to judge, criticize, and rationalize, for it puts us all together at the foot of the Cross. Here we are equal, for none is perfect. Here we receive the daily cleansing Jesus offers. Here we learn to empathize with others who fail, so we say with genuine humility, "There, but for God's grace, go I."

Any quest for personal power and authority only gets in His way. I may feel more capable than someone else for a certain job or role, but my Shepherd usually prefers to work through my weaknesses rather than my strengths.[34] When I see reality from His eternal perspective, He frees me from the pursuit of human praise and admiration. "I count all things loss," said Paul, "for the excellence of the knowledge of Christ Jesus my Lord, for whom I have suffered the loss of all things, and count them as rubbish, that I may gain Christ and be found in Him. . . ."[35]

God's kindness amazes me, but He seldom empowers our work if we refuse to accept His choice and place for us. He knows best where we belong. "For we are His workmanship, created in Christ Jesus for good works, which God prepared beforehand that we should walk in them."[36] His Word helps us find those "good works," and His boundaries keep us close to Him.

The essential questions boil down to a simple choice: What do I value most — human pleasure and power, or God's daily strength and approval for all eternity? Either way, life will be full of challenges — and all the more so as our culture sheds the values that kept us safe. But when we pursue His values and not our own, He will be our shelter. His promise is as true now as it was in Isaiah's days:

> Fear not, for I have redeemed you; I have summoned you by name; you are mine. When you pass through the waters, I will be with you. . . . When you walk through the fire, you will not be burned. . . . For I am the Lord, your God, the Holy One of Israel, your Savior . . . you are precious and . . . I love you (Isa. 43:1-4).

Hold on to that promise, for you will surely pass through fires. Evil exists, no matter how hard people try to imagine it away. "Therefore hear this," continued Isaiah,

> *You who are* given to pleasures, who dwell
> securely, who say in your heart, "I *am,* and *there
> is* no one else besides me. . . ." You have trusted
> in your wickedness; You have said, "No one sees
> me." . . . Therefore evil shall come upon you . . .
> you will not be able to put it off (Isa. 47:8-11).

One of Satan's most destructive temptations is to demean God, prompting us to challenge His wisdom with questions such as this: "If God is both sovereign and good, how can He allow evil?" God *is* both sovereign and full of love — and He does allow evil! The next chapter will show why — and how to triumph over it.

Endnotes

[1] Re-Imagining Conference Tape 1-1, Side B.

[2] Manuela Dunn Mascetti, *The Song of Eve* (New York, NY: Simon & Schuster, 1990), p. 234.

[3] "Weaving Our Wisdom Together," a brochure from Women's Alliance, Oakland, CA.

[4] Organized by the Gorbachev Foundation, the five-day State of the World Forum convened in San Francisco on September 27. The former head of the Communist empire had gathered "nearly 500 senior statespeople, political leaders, spiritual leaders, scientists, intellectuals, business executives, artists, and youth from 50 nations to begin a process of deliberation on the central question of what priorities, values, and actions should guide humanity as it moves into the next phase of development," said Jim Garrison, president of the Gorbachev Foundation. "Human interdependence," he continued, "must now become our watchword as we move into the global civilization which lies ahead: interdependence with each other, interdependence with the earth, interdependence with the Spirit which perennially guides the affairs of humankind."

[5] Deena Metzger, "Re-vamping the World," *Critique*, Vancouver, BC, Spring 1990, p. 22.

[6] Re-Imagining Conference, Minneapolis, MN, November 4-7, 1993.

[7]Starhawk, *The Spiral Dance* (San Francisco, CA: Harper & Row, 1979), p. 23.

[8]Metzger, p. 23.

[9]Robin D. Givhan, "Freely Female," *Detroit Free Press,* August 25, 1991.

[10]Ibid.

[11]See chapter 3. A good resource on Native American spirituality is Clark Wissler's, *Indians of the United States* (New York, NY: Anchor Book, 1940), p. 70-71.

[12]Among the books authored by St. Olaf College faculty and endorsed and reviewed on page 5 in *St.Olaf* (November/December 1994), were *The Limits of Scripture: Vivekananda's Reinterpretation of the Vedas* by Anantanand Rambachan, a religion faculty member; and *Consciousness and the Mind of God* by Charles Taliaferro, which offers "a holistic understanding of the dualist person-body relationship." Rambachan leads a weekly Hindu fellowship for Hindu students and others interested in Eastern spirituality.

[13]Romans 1:32.

[14]Habakkuk 1:3. See also Habakkuk 1:13; Revelation 2:2, 2:20;NIV.

[15]Cited by class "hand-out" from Richard J. Foster, *Renovaré:* Devotional Readings (Vol. 1, no. 43, 1991), no page number shown.

[16]Kenneth Leech, *Soul Friend: An Invitation to Spiritual Direction* (San Francisco, CA: HarperSanFrancisco, 1992), p. 146. Leech cites Julian's *Revelations of Divine Love*, p. 35, 37-39. These pages don't match the translations I have examined. The closest translation I could find was *Julian of Norwich: Showings* (New York, NY: Paulist Press, 1978) translated by Edmund Colledge, p. 154: "God also showed me that sin is no shame, but honour to man. . . . It is to them no shame that they have sinned — shame is not more in the bliss of heaven — for there the tokens of sin are turned into honours." These words are taken out of context; they do not reflect Julian's overall view of sin. However they do show how certain passages are being used to validate the feminist concept of sin.

[17]Ibid., p. 147. Leech cites pages 59-61 in *Divine Revelations*, but again, these page numbers do not match the translations I found. Instead, I would like to cite a few similar quotes from *Julian of Norwich: Showings* (detailed above): "As truly as God is our Father, so truly is God our Mother, and he revealed that in everything, and especially in these sweet words where he says, 'I am he . . . the power and goodness of fatherhood; I am he, the wisdom and the lovingkindness of motherhood. . . . I am he, the Trinity; I am he, the unity; I am he, the great supreme goodness of every kind of thing. . . . As truly as God is our Father, so truly is God our Mother. Our Father wills, our Mother works, our good Lord the Holy Spirit confirms." (p. 295-6).

"Julian also wrote, "The second person of the Trinity is our Mother in nature . . . in whom we are founded and rooted, and he is our Mother of mercy in taking our sensuality. . . . So our Mother works in mercy on all his beloved children who are docile and obedient to him" (p. 294). "So our Lady is our mother, in whom we are all enclosed and born of her in Christ, for she who is mother of our saviour is mother of all who are saved in our saviour; and our saviour is our true Mother, in whom we are endlessly born and out of whom we shall never come" (p. 292).

[18]Romans 6:11-23.

[19]Philip Yancey, "The Lost Sex Study," *Christianity Today*, December 12, 1994, p. 80.

[20]Ibid.

[21]Ibid.

[22]Lester Kirkendall, *Sexuality and Man*, a collection of articles written and compiled by SIECUS board members.

[23]Haven Bradford Gow, "Consequences of Sexual Revolution," *Christian News*, July 3, 1995.

[24]Ibid.

[25]Associated Press, "Experts Say New Generation Is in Trouble Already," *San Francisco Chronicle*, June 9, 1990.

[26]Stanley K. Monteith, "Anticipated Worldwide Death Toll: 1 Billion People," *HIV-Watch* (Vol. II, No. 1), p. 7.

[27]Romans 6:12.

[28]A. J. Hostetler, "Three-Quarters of Female Smokers Say They Want to Quit, But Can't," *Christian News*, February 27, 1995.

[29]George Will, "Moral Sense Ability," *San Jose Mercury News*, December 20, 1993.

[30]William K. Kilpatrick, "Turning Out Moral Illiterates," *Los Angeles Times, July 20, 1993*.

[31]The title of a wonderful daily devotional by Oswald Chambers.

[32]Luke 4:4.

[33]Galatians 2:20.

[34]2 Corinthians 4:7-11, 12:9-10.

[35]Philippians 3:8-9.

[36]Ephesians 2:10.

Chapter 8

Deliver Us from Evil,
or
There Is No Sin or Evil?

❧

Evil is back. (Cover of *New York Times Magazine*)

Your constant crusading against sin makes everyone feel guilty. We've voted to let you go. (A cartoon showing board members looking accusingly at their director)

Remove God from a throne in the sky and place God where God is — in everything we call good, in that which we call evil and certainly in that which we call the human mind. It is time we begin to see God not as other but as ourselves. (Deborah Turner-Bey, *Creation Spirituality*)[1]

We are of God . . . [but] the whole world lies under the sway of the wicked one. (1 John 5:19)

❧

Years ago, I picked up a free magazine called *Well-Being Journal* in a health food store. I threw it away a few days later, but I may never forget a comment I read. Apparently, the author had received this bit of wisdom from her inner guide: "Many people believe in evil, sin, and dark forces. It is your purpose to teach the opposite which is the Truth: there is no devil, no hell, no sin, no guilt except in the creative mind of humankind."[2]

That people believe this lie suits the devil just fine. He has always tried to blur our view of evil and our sensitivity to sin. C.S. Lewis said it well:

> There are two equal and opposite errors into which our race can fall about the devils. One is to disbelieve in their existence. The other is to believe, and to feel an excessive and unhealthy interest in them.[3]

Neo-pagans do both. Most would deny the existence of Satan and his army of demons. Yet, they believe in them, for the nature spirits they trust for insight are nothing but demons masquerading as helpful guides and angelic friends.

While the evidence for supernatural evil multiplies all around us, more and more people deny it. Sure, they may believe in cosmic forces and bad vibes. But sin or Satan? They don't fit the new paradigm.

In October 1995, our local school district held a large public meeting to discuss Halloween festivities. Most parent were angry at some proposed limitations on the traditional in-school celebration of a "harmless holiday." Why worry about the small minority who felt offended by its ancient link to a dead religion?

Only a few minority voices were heard. A former Wiccan priest explained that the old Celtic witchcraft that gave birth to Halloween is anything but dead. Flourishing in today's pagan revival, it has become an official religion with tax-exempt status.[4] A few parents shared their concerns about programs that compelled children to celebrate occult themes. They knew well that pagan symbols and occult amusement were desensitizing children to a fast-spreading subculture obsessed with death, spells, and black magic — not just at Halloween but all year long.[5]

The majority booed, jeered, and refused to listen. "These are religious objections to secular events," declared the president of the board, Phil Faillaice. Everyone seemed to have forgotten that a different minority had, only nine months earlier, banned Christmas songs as offensive to *their* beliefs. But times have changed. By the end of the evening, the pro-Halloween group had won its case, and the media spread the "good" news from coast to coast.

"We have the holiday back again," declared Bay Area witch, Zsuzsanna Budapest. "These pagan calendars are imprinted in our genes. They cannot be taken away."

"It's hard to give up a good party," added Daniel Melia, UC Berkeley professor of Celtic languages. "Satan is a Christian notion. This is a pre-Christian celebration."[6]

He is wrong about Satan. The Old Testament mentions Satan 14 times, and that doesn't include all his other names. From beginning to end, the Bible shows how Lucifer has always been stirring rebellion against God and hatred for His people. But then as now, the good news outshines the bad: the evil one could never cause more trouble than God would allow.[7]

The clash between two cultures at Halloween is part of the war raging in the unseen, and the enemy's strategy hasn't changed since the Old Testament days when God warned, "Woe to those who call evil good, and good evil; who put darkness for light, and light for darkness" (Isa. 5:20). Year after year, Satan keeps on trying to trick us into believing the opposite. As Bibles gather dust, his influence multiplies.

Remember how Pat was "delivered from the power of darkness" and transferred "into the kingdom" of God? Before she learned God's Word, she had no resistance to Satan's lies. Now she knows with the rest of us that "we are of God, and [that] *the whole world lies under the sway of the wicked one.*"[8] Satan's influence is no small force to reckon with, and we had better know the enemy we face each day:

> For we do not wrestle against flesh and blood, but against principalities, against powers, against the rulers of the darkness of this age, against spiritual *hosts* of wickedness in the heavenly *places* (Eph. 6:11-12).

Those who don't love God, cannot "stand firm" against the "wiles of the devil."[9] As Ephesians 2 warns us, they "walk according to the prince of the power of the air, the spirit who now works in the sons of disobedience. . . ." Anyone not part of God's kingdom will be swayed by Satan's armies which have fine-tuned their skills. That's why there is evil in the world — and why it intensifies when people turn from God's love to Satan's seductive evil.

Few understand Satan's schemes better than Valerie Duffy, the former witch whom you met in chapter 6. "The feast of Samhain (sah-ween) is an unholy Sabbath observed by occultists worldwide," she explains. Freed from the demonic forces that once controlled her life, she now lives in an "upstate New York" community that often publicizes Wiccan coven meetings and "full moon" celebrations. Each October, she fights — and wins — a spiritual battle against oppressive forces that intensify their attacks near the Wiccan holiday.[10]

Valerie knows all too well why neo-pagans love Halloween. The old Celtic "sabbat" is their main feast — a window of time when the walls between the physical and spiritual worlds supposedly become thin enough to allow easy crossovers. This was the time to catch up with one's ancestors and other spirits from the underworld.[11] But don't think the Vigil of Samhain was just a fun holiday. The "Lord of the Dead," Samhain himself, is no deity to laugh at. Valerie explains why:

> On October 31, black-cloaked druids bearing torches would go door-to-door to select hu-

mans for their New Year's sacrifice to the Lord of the Dead. In return for the child or infant, they would leave a hollowed turnip with candle light shining through the carved face — a satanic counterfeit for the biblical Passover.

In the reveling that took place on that night to Samhain, the demons supposedly loosed for the night would pass over the homes "marked" by the carved lantern. Those families had provided the required gift or sacrifice. Other homes could be hit — sometimes with sudden death.

The children selected for sacrifice were tossed into a bonfire. The druids called it a bone-fire since only the bones were left. From the agonizing screams of the dying, the divining priests would foretell the future of the village.[12]

Does the last statement sound familiar? Remember how the shaman or medicine man in Disney's *Pocahontas* read the future in the smoke from his ritual fire. When you look behind today's idealized images of the world's pagan religions, you find some awesome similarities. Small wonder since Satan, the mastermind behind the druid rituals, usually repeats the same basic strategies wherever he works.

SATAN	
Genesis 3:1-7	Twists truth to seduce God's people
1 Chronicles 21:1	Prompts people to sin
Isaiah 14:12-14	Determines to "be like the Most High"
Luke 4:13	Waits for "opportune" times when we are vulnerable
Luke 8:12	Snatches truth from our hearts
Luke 13:16	Puts people in bondage
Luke 22:3	Can enter into those who betray Christ

Evil Is Back

Throughout history, whenever God's people would trade truth for myth, they slid back into decadence.[13] Today we see the same downward trend reflected in newspaper headlines such as these:

- Senseless Slayings Baffle Police
- Phone Sex Industry . . . Going Overseas
- Teen Gambling Is the Latest Addiction of Choice
- Youth Sex Offenders Younger Than Ever
- Racial Tension at Colleges: Shocking but Real
- Teen Gangs Vandalize Suburbs
- Girl, 14, Slays 2 Boys and Self
- Nine Texas Children Admit Torturing Horse

Some of the most shocking stories deal with children who run wild. Lacking any sense of shame, three teenage boys stabbed, strangled, and beat a 55-year-old man crippled by multiple sclerosis — then feasted on the spaghetti in his refrigerator. He "didn't have a chance," concluded the *Newsweek* story. "The boys who allegedly attacked him . . . were ruthless."[14]

Girls are fast catching up with boys. In New Orleans, a 13-year-old schoolgirl pulled out a knife and plunged it into a classmate's back. "You name the crime, we have it; you think about the worst scenarios and we have them here," said Edward Cue, an official with California's "hard core" Youth Authority School in Ventura.[15]

The lack of remorse baffles law officers. Why are both children and adults losing the old sensitivity to the horrors of evil? Why can't they tell right from wrong?

The *New York Times* cover story that declared "evil is back," raised the same questions: "What does it mean? Violence? Mindless wickedness? Malignant wickedness?"[16]

The answer is: all the above. People love evil. Children gleefully watch televised death scenes that might have shocked hardened spectators in the old Roman coliseum. The lure of cruelty, violence, and occult horrors sell some of the most popular children's books as well as supermarket tabloids. By its mere exposure and availability, evil has been reinvented. Now it feels good, not bad — exciting, not repulsive. And Satan grins.

Fictionalized evil separates people from the reality of human suffering, which is just what the evil one intended. Many become spectators rather than participants in real community life. Eventually, both real and imagined violence becomes significant only as entertainment.

Some years ago, a car hit an elderly couple in a busy shopping complex. A crowd was already gathering at the scene when I happened to come by. It didn't take long to see the streams of blood from both their heads, yet no one had bound their wounds or covered their shivering bodies. I cried out for blankets or jackets, scarves — anything to stop the bleeding and slow the shock. Nobody responded — neither men nor women. When I tried to stop the bleeding from the woman's broken skull with a tissue from my purse, the spectators just stared with blank faces. I called to the owner of the car for a blanket or clothing. He didn't move. When I ran to his car and grabbed some dry cleaned clothes from his back seat, he protested. I suppose he didn't want blood on his clean clothes. Eventually an ambulance came and took the victims away.

What happened to the Christian compassion that once built hospitals for the world's hungry and sick?

The Bible mentions people who act like animals. "What's wrong with that?" some might argue. "Animals are nicer than people."

Those who study animals see the harsh nature behind the soft fur, brown eyes, and flattering media images. An anthropologist had been studying a group of monkeys for some time when a party of chimpanzees invaded the territory. "The results were devastating," he wrote. "During the hour-long hunt, seven [monkeys] were killed; three were torn apart in front of me. Nearly four hours later, the hunters were still eating . . . while I sat staring in disbelief at the remains of many of my study subjects."[17]

Were These Animals Evil?

No. Evil is unique to humanity. We alone are given a moral choice and God's Word to help us resist temptation. Animals are expected to follow their natural instincts, but humans are held accountable to God's standard. Ignorance of that standard doesn't cancel the consequences for not heeding it. "They are without excuse," the Bible tells us.[18]

America seems embarrassed to talk about God's standard these days. We're ashamed of what He calls good, but we "don't even know how to blush" at what He calls sin.[19] No wonder evil is rampant and people are desensitized to evil, horror, and human suffering.

I stopped by a large bookstore one day and discovered a huge new display inside. Startled, I stared at a child-sized open casket filled with vampire books. The wooden casket was leaning against a large imitation stone altar. On it, stood an embellished cross with candles on each side. In the center, displayed like a Bible, lay a large book. Horrified at the mockery of Christianity, I checked the cover and found *Memnoch the Devil,* the latest top-selling vampire book by Anne Rice. On the gray cathedral-like wall above the altar hung a cross. I hurried out of the store.

The Two Sides of Evil

Imaginary horror not only desensitizes us to God's good, it opens people to real demonic horrors and deadly occult bondage. Yet, bad as overt occultism is, neo-paganism is far more seductive and just as effective for Satan's purposes today. Both paths link human minds directly to the realm of demons. Both lead to the same devastating end. But all too often, neo-paganism looks deceptively light and kind.

Johanna Michaelson showed its enticing side in her eye-opening book *The Beautiful Side of Evil*. Her exploration into the realm of psychic surgery uncovered demonic activities far more horrible than the diseases they supposedly healed.

Some years ago, I talked with a nurse involved with holistic medicine. Jane and her husband had learned an holistic form of massage therapy that seemed to relieve her back pain, at least for a while. Like the Chinese *ch'i* and the Hindu *prana* (taught at the Re-Imagining Conference), a spiritual force would flow through their hands, bringing healing by balancing their energies. But as the time passed, Jane grew more and more dependent on her husband's treatment. Each time he massaged, the pain would fade. But the pain-free periods between massages grew shorter while the pain that soon followed grew more intense. She became desperate for lasting relief.

Lying in bed one night, Jane sensed something dark approach her. Terrified, she cried out, "In the name of Jesus, get out of here!" The unearthly presence left, but Jane and her husband realized that something was terribly wrong. What had they done to invite this kind of demonic manifestation?

After a brief search, they found a pastor who helped them understand the occult links to holistic healing. Like Valerie, they had to confess, renounce, and stop all the practices they had learned to trust. Guess what happened to Jane's back? God healed it. When she chose to trust Him, He set her free.

Please don't think that all illness is demonic and can end so quickly. God can heal any of us in a moment, but He seldom chooses the smoothest path for us. Sometimes prolonged illness becomes our best opportunity to demonstrate His overcoming life and peace to others.

The point of the above story is: what seems so good may prove very dangerous. It's not easy to tell the difference. Without God's Word as our standard or reference point, it is impossible. Remember, Satan counterfeits every good gift God has given us.

Nothing blurs that line more than today's popular angels. "What idea is more beguiling than the notion of lithesome spirits, free of time and space and human weakness, hovering between us and all harm?" asks Nancy Gibbs in *Time* magazine's 1993 cover story "Angels Among Us."[20]

"They're non-threatening, wise, and loving beings," says Eileen Freeman, publisher of a bimonthly newsletter called *Angel Watch.* "They offer help whether we ask for it or not."[21]

Since angels abound in the world's pagan religions as well as in biblical history, they fit the need for multi-cultural gods. Sophy Burnham, who has studied Buddhism and Hinduism and written the two bestsellers, *A Book of Angels* and *Angel Letters,* say they blend the "best parts" of many religions. "People are looking for hope," she says. "In the media, we hear of so much horror and despair. But angels make us know we are loved — these wonderful beings are protecting us."[22]

And how do you contact these sweet feminine helpers? "It's simple," said Ms. Burham. You simply "go inside yourself. . . . Then you ask for what you need, you sit back, and you wait. It will come."[23]

Today, *it* probably will. As Alma Daniels points out in her best-seller *Ask Your Angels,* everything has changed. Whereas in pagan cultures, only the shaman or medicine man had direct contact with the spirit world, now everyone can be led by their personal demon. She explains,

> We stand on the brink of a massive change.
> On the one hand, we face apparent global disaster,
> and on the other there is the potential for the most
> glorious spiritual transformation our species has
> ever seen. . . .

At this time of personal and planetary acceleration, previous rules and old forms are being discarded. *Contact with the angels, which used to take years of meditation and dedication, is now available to all who seek it,* because the angels are closer to us, and more open to working with us on a conscious level, than they have been in thousands of years. . . .

The angels aren't making contact just with special people, or in a secret way. They are doing it openly, joyfully.[24] (Emphasis added)

"There was a time when I was on a quest for power, knowledge, and alliance with unseen powers," said my friend Jane Gorevin, an Oregon mother. "I discovered a multitude of angelic beings within a spiritual hierarchy, each with distinct character, area of influence, and level of power. My mind and power was no match for these forces, but God was! He enabled me to see behind the seductive masks into the face of willful, malignant evil."

"Angels, both good and evil, have been present since the beginning of time," Jane continued. "God's angels serve as ministering spirits to His people. Fallen angels masquerade as caring helpers — but only until they accomplish their purpose. In reality, they hate everyone, even each other. I finally renounced the forces of Satan, then God showed me genuine love — something 'the angel of light' can never counterfeit."[25]

Demons that masquerade as angels love to twist and distort God's truths and whisper deadly advice into their subjects' ears. They are evil, not good, and we need to know the difference. Use God's Word as your standard, and study the following chart.

Two Kinds of Angels	
God's Angels	**Fallen Angels**
Accountable to God (Job 2:1)	Oppose God
Sent by God (Exod. 23:20)	Requested by humans
Respond to God's will (Psalm 91:11)	Respond to rituals (at *their* will)
God chooses which angel (Matt. 18:10)	We choose our favorite angel
Fulfills God's will (Luke 4:10)	Fulfill our will (at first)
Speaks in the name of God (Luke 1:28)	Speak like us (if they choose)
Brings awe, respect, fear (Luke 1:11-13)	Appear friendly and natural like us

Did you notice the similarity between angels and the self-made goddesses in chapters 2 and 3? Remember that people who create their own deities usually imagine them in their own image. No wonder, then, that today's angelic goddesses reflect their maker's noble dreams and human cravings. Designed with a little help from the "angels," they have become alluringly approachable.

We all want an accessible God who loves us as we are. The true God fits that need, but the evil one is always trying to tell us otherwise. His goal is to draw us to himself so that he, not the Holy Spirit, will guide our thoughts and actions. And since Satan can tailor-make his counterfeits to match Christian as well as pagan wants, even committed Christians are vulnerable.

Deceiving Spirits

The shift from a truth-based Christianity to a feeling-based spirituality has swung wide the door to deception. Today, if a teacher or "prophet" majors in manifestations rather than biblical truth — or if anyone suggests that you seek an *experience* rather than a deep understanding of God through His Word — beware.[26] God wants you to delight in His presence, but seeking ecstatic *experiences* rather than oneness with His heart and purpose can lead to deception.

My British friend Tricia learned this lesson the hard way. During a time of loneliness many years ago, she tried to visualize Jesus and *feel* His presence. But instead of meeting the biblical God, a demonic spirit came to her posing as Jesus. As the months went by, she kept using visualization to invoke the actual presence of what seemed to be a loving divine being. The feeling that came over her "seemed not in the slightest evil," she says. "It seemed full of love and peace."

At first, she couldn't believe that this presence might be deceiving her. *What nonsense! Of course I can feel the love of God!* she thought when a book she was reading suggested that the experience could be demonic. "I wasn't prepared to let it go," she explained later. "It already had me bound."

Tricia pondered the warnings as she kept reading the book. Yes, God desires her love, but not just warm bodily feelings or ecstatic emotions. He seeks a love that is committed to knowing His Word and serving His people. Finally another experience confirmed her growing concern. "I lay in bed one morning and the same presence came over me," she said. "Suddenly I felt as if I were floating in the air. I don't know if I actually lifted off the bed or levitated, but it certainly felt that way!

This surely isn't right, she thought. In the name of Jesus, she told anything that was not of God to leave, and immediately the sensation faded. The deceiving spirit never returned, and Tricia committed herself afresh to the true

God and His Word. Never will she forget the warning in 1 John 4:1: "Do not believe every spirit, but test the spirits, whether they are of God."[27]

Did you notice the similarities between Tricia's story, and those of Pat and Valerie? (See chapters 3 and 6.) All describe encounters with demons disguised as God. What made Tricia's story different was her relationship to God. She was already joined to Jesus Christ and loving His Word. The counterfeit spirit inspired her through its outer presence, not its inner guidance. Instead of enslaving her, the demon tried to block her effectiveness for God. Pat and Valerie, on the other hand, were being trained as effective servants for the domain of darkness.

Personal encounters with "Jesus" and "angels" are becoming more common — just as Alma Daniels predicted. Even in churches caught up in this movement, few take time to "test the spirits." So when Marianne Williamson, who popularized A Course in Miracles, cloaks her occultism in biblical terms, church women listen. "We spiritually reconstitute our lives by asking Him to enter us," she says referring to a pantheistic God. "We ask Him into every situation . . . to change dramatically our orientation."[28]

Few authors have changed our spiritual orientation more than Betty Eadie who wrote Embraced by the Light. During her supposed "near-death" experience[29] she met a loving "Jesus" who appeared "more brilliant than the sun."[30] With three "angels" as her guides, she was shown an occult spiritual system that fused her Mormon and Native American heritage with contemporary New Age teachings. Her supposedly "Christian" experience contradicts the Bible on every point. Who do you think was her source of "wisdom"?

Many people see near-death experiences as opportunities to preview heaven.[31] Few know the darker side. In pagan cultures, shamans often "met" their personal animal spirit (spirit guide or demon) during childhood near-death experiences which opened doors to demonic spirits and visions.

Apparently, Betty Eadie did. During a serious illness after her mother, a "full-blooded Sioux Indian," had left her at a boarding school, the girl slipped into a coma. While in this trance-like state, she saw a spiritual being whose beard sparkled with light.[32] "Most shamans receive an 'initiatory call' . . . during a personal illness serious enough to induce a coma (a form of trance)," wrote William Lyon in his biography of Indian shaman Black Elk.

Unlike Christian families who come under God's protection, tribal cultures are driven by superstitions, fears, and rituals that buy protection from certain powerful spirits or demons against more frightening ones. Today the same occult rituals merge with all kinds of occult arts and teachings. "Angels are firmly rooted in the collective unconscious of the human race," writes Geoffrey James, who looks at angels through the filter of Jungian psychology. "Their energy can be tapped by practicing the Western magical system of Angel Magic . . . a practical application of the cabal (or kabbala, an ancient form of Jewish occultism), tarot, and astrology."[34]

Evil is back by popular demand. And while, Satan, masquerading as "an angel of light," can only oppress Christians to the extent God allows,[35] He has all the rest of humanity to trap and train as counterfeit "ministers of righteousness."[36] Their main work is to turn people away from God and link them to the occult. (Nothing fits their plan better than "Christians" who receive their lies and proclaim them to others as prophecies from God.) Most of these "ministers" fit one of the following levels of service:

1. *Pagan priests, shamans, spiritists, and New Age teachers* — people who actively seek to harness occult powers and lead others into the occult.

2. *Followers and supporters* — those who promote the new spirituality and participate in its rituals.

3. The deceived masses — those who flow with the social changes and deny the realities of God.

4. So-called Christians without a personal relationship with Christ — those who bear Christ's name but don't follow His ways. They serve Satan by discrediting Christ outside the church and confusing Christians inside the church.[37]

Deliver Us from Evil

The subtle effects of Satan's schemes can be seen in the questions we ask and the answers we give. Some years ago, a news reporter asked two "theological questions": What caused Susan Smith, who shocked the nation by drowning her two young sons, to commit this "evil deed"? And why did God permit it?

People can guess, but only God has the answers. Since we cannot understand ourselves until we learn to understand God, the last question must come first: He gives people free choice. Susan, who followed her confused feelings, made the wrong choice.

Those answers may sound harsh to people who don't understand God's longing to comfort and heal sinners. The world prefers to rationalize (my culture made me do it), excuse (I was born with the wrong genes), and blame (my parents abused me), none of which provide practical answers to inexplicable evil. To the perplexed public, Susan looked "less like the perpetrator than the victim," wrote the reporter. "She was the victim of an 'irresistible impulse,' she had no choice, it really wasn't her act, it really wasn't her. . . ."[38]

Those excuses eliminate the only compassionate solution since sin, Satan, evil, and death can't be imagined away. When people refuse to see or admit their failures, the Cross can't help them. Jesus was crucified for individual sinners, not for the collective guilt of a dysfunctional society. He saves us one by one, and He loves us each as unique persons.

Those who have walked through His door of deliverance know that well. You saw how Valerie's life changed. The last seven years of her life haven't been easy, but they have been filled with peace in the midst of turmoil, exciting victories after spiritual battles, and daily fellowship with the God who became her best friend.

No one has ever been immune to Satan's torments and temptations — not even the apostle Paul. But when he looked at his struggles from God's perspective, he saw how God used evil for His good purpose. And when he saw how pride could have blocked his vision of God, he welcomed the pain that made him strong:

> Lest I should be exalted above measure by the abundance of the revelations, a thorn in the flesh was given to me, a messenger of Satan to buffet me.... I pleaded with the Lord three times that it might depart from me. And He said to me, "My grace is sufficient for you, for My strength is made perfect in weakness." Therefore most gladly I will rather boast in my infirmities, that the power of Christ may rest upon me. Therefore I take pleasure in infirmities, in reproaches, in needs, in persecutions, in distresses, for Christ's sake. For when I am weak, then I am strong (2 Cor. 12:7-12).

I understand what he is talking about. Disappointments, divisions, slander, and persecution often break our hearts and test our faith as we try to serve our King. Yet they serve God's purpose, for they help us see the malignancy of what God calls evil. Better yet, they also prompt us to trust God rather than our feelings, to exercise the faith and discipline needed to respond with love, and to make every effort to avoid the consequences of tolerating evil.[39] Thus evil, when seen from His perspective, becomes a catalyst to make us strong in Christ, not in ourselves.[40]

As we come to Him in humility, gratefulness, surrender, and obedience — the exact opposite of what feminism demands — He reminds us that the hurtful things that touch our lives keep us where we long to be: close to himself at the foot of the cross. There, each morning, we can give Him our lives, our minds, our plans, and all the struggles that would distract and defeat us that day. Freed from the lures of resentment and self-pity and filled with His life and peace, we can say with Paul, "God forbid that I should boast except in the cross of our Lord Jesus Christ, by whom the world has been crucified to me, and I to the world" (Gal. 6:14).

Hidden in Christ, we are ready to face evil in His strength. Like Jesus, we have the Word of God, which "is living and powerful, sharper than any two-edged sword" (Heb. 4:12). When we speak it in faith, it cuts through the veil of illusions, shows us the truth, and frees us from the seductive pull of the particular evil that might have corrupted our thoughts and defeated our witness:

> For the weapons of our warfare *are* not carnal but mighty in God for pulling down strongholds, casting down arguments and every high thing that exalts itself against the knowledge of God, bringing every thought into captivity to the obedience of Christ (2 Cor. 10:4-5).

Notice the last part. New thoughts and arguments that oppose God's Word on every point are driving the feminist movement. The next chapter will show where the worldwide sisterhood is heading and why its victory would devastate, not save, the world.

Endnotes

[1]Deborah Turner-Bye, "Our Dark Mother's Children," *Creation Spirituality* (November/December 1993), p. 13.

[2]This magazine was probably published in 1992.

[3]C.S. Lewis, *The Screwtape Letters* (New York, NY: Bantam Books, 1995), p. xiii.

[4]"Witches use taxes to gain public OK," *The Journal* (Providence, RI), August 14, 1989.

[5]While the Bible warns against any contact with witchcraft, magic, spells, and spiritism (Deut. 18:9-12), the obsession with occult books and games (Magic Gathering, Dungeons and Dragons, occult computer games) and youthful covens of witches practicing black magic, is multiplying from coast to coast.

[6]Annie Nakao, "Pagan Ways Live On," *San Francisco Examiner*, October 22, 1995.

[7]Job 1 shows how Satan had to ask permission. . . . God reigns, and He always does what He pleases. Therefore some who don't understand His ways, blame Him for evil or call Him weak for not ending it. How can you eliminate evil without turning humans into puppets without any free will?

[8]1 John 5:19

[9]Ephesians 6:10-13.

[10]The spiritual battle is won through memorizing, trusting, speaking, and living God's Word. Valerie "puts on the full armor of God" (see Eph. 6:10-18 and the chart at the end of chapter 2.

[11]Margot Adler, *Drawing Down the Moon* (Boston, MA: Beacon Press, 1979), p. 110.

[12]Merle Severy, "The Celts," *National Geographic* (May 1977), p. 625-626, describes "the eve of Samhain . . . the start of the Celtic new year: "According to the Dinshenchas, a medieval collection of "the lore of prominent places," firstborn children were sacrificed before a great idol to ensure fertility of cattle and crops. Samhain eve was a night of dread and danger. At this juncture of the old year and the new, our world and the otherworld opened up to each other. The dead returned, ghosts and demons were abroad, and the future could be seen. . . . Behind such Halloween games as bobbing for apples lie Celtic divination arts to discern who would marry, thrive, or die in the coming year. Behind the masks and mischief, the jack-o' lanterns, and food offerings lurk the fear of malevolent spirits and the rites to propitiate them." Page 601 gives additional insight: "Tacitus tells us of the bloodstained Druid altars of Anglesey in Wales. Caesar describes mass human sacrifice in Gaul: 'Some of the tribes make colossal wickerwork figures, the limbs of which are filled with living men; these images are then set alight and the victims perish in a sea of flame.' " For more general information about Celtic religion and Samhain, see *Encyclopedia Britannica*.

[13]Read the book of Judges, 2 Kings, 2 Chronicles, Isaiah, Jeremiah, and research the downward slide of Greek and Roman civilization.

[14]Barbara Kantrowitz, "Wild in the Streets," *Newsweek* (August 2, 1993); 40.

[15]Connie Leslie, "Girls Will be Girls," *Newsweek* (August 2, 1993), p. 44.

[16]Ron Rosenbaum, "Staring into the Heart of Darkness," *New York Times Magazine* (June 4, 1995); 36.

[17]"The Circle of Death," *The American Enterprise* (September/October 1995), p. 11.

[18]Romans 1:19-20

[19]Jeremiah 6:15, 8:12.

[20]Nancy Gibbs, "Angels Among Us," *Time* (December 27, 1993), p. 56.

[21]Ibid.

[22]Dawn Raffel, "Angels All Around Us," *Redbook* (December 1992), p. 92.

[23]Craig Wilson, "Hark and Hallelujah! The Angels are Here," *San Jose Mercury News*, October 28, 1992.

[24]Alma Daniel, Timothy Wyllie, Andrew Ramer, *Ask Your Angel* (New York, NY: Ballatine Books, 1992), p. 22.

[25]From telephone conversations and Jane Gorevin's personal letter to me.

[26]See Deuteronomy 13:1-5, 18:15-22; Matthew 24:11, 24; Mark 13:22; 2 Peter 2:1; 1 John 4:1.

[27]From testimony sent to me by Tricia Tillen.

[28]Marianne Williamson, "Speak to the One Who Loves You the Best," *Body Mind Spirit*, March 1995, p. 55.

[29]It had not been medically validated when she wrote her book.

[30]Betty J. Eadie, *Embraced by the Light* (Placerville, CA: Gold Leaf Press, 1992), p. 41.

[31]To understand both near-death experiences and *Embraced by the Light*, read Doug Groothuis' well-documented book *Deceived by the Light* (Eugene, OR: Harvest House Publishers, 1995).

[32]Eadie, p. 4-5.

[33]Wallace Black Elk and William S. Lyon, *Black Elk: The Sacred Ways of a Lakota* (New York, NY: HarperCollins Publishers, 1991), p. xviii.

[34]"Get the Real Story on Angel Power," *Llewellyn's New Worlds of Mind and Spirit*, October/November, 1995, p. 24.

[35]Job 1:10; Deuteronomy 23:14; Ezra 9:9; Psalm 5:11, 32:7, 91:14-15; John 17:11-15; 2 Thessalonians 3:3; 2 Peter 2:5-10.

[36]2 Corinthians 11:14-15.

[37]See Matthew 7:18; 13:24-40; James 3:1-12.

[38]Rosenbaum, 36.

[39]Romans 1:28-32.

[40]Matthew 5:11; 13:41; Hebrews 12:5-12; 1 Peter 4:2; 2 Peter 1:4; Proverbs 16:4;NAS, Ezekiel 20:24.

Chapter 9

Yours Is the Power, or Mine Is the Power?

❧

I am power! I am power! (A chant led by Bella Abzug at U.N.'s World Conference for Women)

The female liberation movement is developing in the context of international social revolution." Sisterhood Is Powerful[1]

*I did not . . . rise again on the third day to show you what I could do, but what **you** can do. Yours is the power. Yours is the glory! (*Barbara Marx Hubbard's message from the spirit she calls Christ)[2]

I am the Lord, that is My name; and my glory I will not give to another, nor My praise to carved images. (Isa. 42:8)

❧

"We are all connected!"
That theme, proclaimed from a poster welcoming

women to the June 1995 celebration called "Women and the United Nations," echoed the hope of feminists around the world. Picturing a circle of dancing women, it introduced a new art exhibit which showed "women of all nations celebrating the strengths, diversity, and shared experiences of all women."

It didn't take long to see that the "shared experiences of all women" was pain and oppression. Pictures of sad, angry, contorted, and naked women lined the long bayfront hallway leading to the San Francisco auditorium where women were gathering to discuss the coming United Nations Fourth World Conference on Women.

Matching the theme, an oversized collage featured a nude goddess with hands reaching out to a turbulent, hurting world. Dark faces crying out in agony surrounded her long surrealistic yellow body.

Only a few pictures offered hope. A nude pastel-colored woman symbolized the U.N.'s solution to pain: a worldwide change in consciousness causing humanity to see itself as *one* united people, speaking with *one* voice, and "thinking in common . . . so that the experience of the mass is behind the simple voice."

If the U.N. has its way, that simple, collective voice would be forced to speak *its* ideology. That ideology colored all the promotional literature and gifts offered at the entrance to the auditorium: the campaign buttons that called for "Choice" and the "ERA;" the books and pamphlets promoting Planned Parenthood, NOW; and the American Association of University Women.

I picked up a book titled *Choices* from one of the display tables and scanned the pages. Published by the Angry Isis Press, it was full of caustic cartoons mocking pastors, Christian parents, the Bible, and pro-life activists. Many drawings looked familiar. They were drawn by the creators of syndicated series such as Cathy, Feiffer, Sylvia, and Doonesbury. Apparently, these artists agreed that extramarital sex with freedom from consequences is a woman's right. Any moral or legal deterrent makes her victim of a patriarchal culture ruled by men "trying to control women's bodies."[3]

This was not a happy place. Nor did it welcome men. My husband came as far as the entrance, but noticing the cold stares, he chose to leave. "I hoped he would go somewhere else and let you come in alone," said the women who sold me the $10 ticket.

I looked at the program she gave me. "We have come together," it announced, "to honor the involvement of women," "envision and forecast a future agenda that will include and empower all women," and work together to "end war and dissonance in the world."

Noble goals, I thought to myself, *especially the last one. But how could the United Nations end expressions of disunity except by worldwide totalitarian controls?*

The conference began half an hour late — not bad for U.N.-type meetings. The speakers gave a preview of the upcoming U.N. Conference on Women. About 5,000 official delegates and participants from over 180 nations would meet in Beijing in September 1995 to finish the international document declaring the feminist plan for global transformation of schools, homes, work, and values. Starting a few days earlier, the Non-Governmental Organizations (NGO) would meet in Huairou, about 30 miles away. Across that awkward distance, more than 25,000 NGO participants — representing groups ranging from Planned Parenthood to Focus on the Family — would try to influence the official delegates in Beijing.

Three months later, the Beijing Conference would begin. The pain and oppression felt by women around the world would be re-imagined to fit feminist needs for victims and scapegoats — two essential players in their planned revolution.

Goddesses at the NGO Forum

"We are building a shrine to the goddesses,"[4] announced the leader of a workshop titled "Goddess and Women, Hand in Hand." The shrine would be constructed in the Peace Tent, one of many tents built to house special displays and events.

A shrine to the goddesses? In China, which seemed so hostile to religious expressions? Diane Knippers, president of the Institute on Religion and Democracy,[5] pondered the paradox. When she arrived in Beijing, a flier from the Chinese "Security Committee" warned her to "refrain from staging religious activities or distributing religious publicity material"[6] outside designated areas. She eventually found the place designated for Christians — a dingy structure at the far edge of the conference site. Yet, the Peace Tent was in the center of activities.

"The goddess was everywhere," she explained later. "The opening ceremony of the NGO Forum was held in a giant Olympic Stadium, the end of which boasted a huge steel-gray profile of the Goddess of Joy.'" And women soon filled the Shrine to the Goddesses with all kinds of goddess figurines, pictures, and small statues. Those who had no idol to offer could simply create one on the spot using the handy "paper-doll cut-outs", glue, and glitter.

The star of the NGO was former congresswoman Bella Abzug, head of WEDO (Women's Environmental and Development Organization), the leading feminist NGO. It sponsored a series of meetings called "Daughters of the Earth." Each session was dedicated to a different goddess — Athena, Ishtar, Nu Kwa, Tara, Pasowee, etc.

At the first meeting, a Brazilian leader presented a thank offering of fruit to "Mother Earth." Then she lifted a Christian cross saying, "The people from my community used to believe in the crucifixion but we have decided 'No more crucifixion.' We believe in life!" She began chanting, "We are power. No one empowers anyone, we do this ourselves."

Bella Abzug stood up and the rest followed. Clasping each other's hands, they raised their arms and chanted, "I am power! I am power!"

"Welcome, daughters of the earth," intoned Abzug when the chant died down. Her words echoed the militancy of WEDO's official warcry, "A Woman's Creed":

> We have survived femicide. We have re-belled. . . . We are whale-song and rainforest . . . the lost and despised. . . . The exercise of imagining is an act of creation. The act of creation is an exercise of will. All this is political. And possible. . . . Believe it. We are the women who will transform the world.[7]

Funded in part by the United Methodist Women's Division, WEDO "advocates 50/50 quotas of men and women in all government and policy-making bodies; prefers socialist economic models over free market options; argues against 'traditional family values' and 'fundamentalism' . . . supports 'abortion as a basic method of fertility regulation' and an essential reproductive right; and seeks to indoctrinate children and youth on its understanding of 'women's rights,' "[8] wrote Diane Knippers. Most of these demands were included in the final Beijing Platform for Action. The officials from the U.N., the World Bank, and the International Monetary Fund who joined the last WEDO meeting added their unspoken authority to its revolutionary claims.[9]

WEDO led the march toward feminist power, but countless other groups followed. An "anti-imperialism" parade showed the political mood at the NGO Forum. Its banner bore an ominously familiar slogan: "Down with US Imperialism. Women of the Toiling Class Unite."[10]

No Tolerance for Christians

You may remember that the U.N. dubbed 1995 the "Year of Tolerance." Yet, the narrow tolerance shown in

Beijing excluded all opponents to the feminist agenda. Women could speak freely as long as they fit the planned "consensus," and U.N. organizers would block pro-life groups that tried to "unbalance the proceedings."[11] As Andrei Vishinsky wrote in *The Law of the Soviet State*, "naturally, there can be no place for freedom of speech, press, and so on for the foes of socialism."[12]

"I think . . . those in favor of the Beijing draft platform simply don't want their positions challenged," wrote journalist Michael Miller, "and they're resorting to straw-man arguments, doublespeak, and name-calling."[13] Dissenters were discredited as "extremist religious groups." When asked for an example of an "extremist" group, a member of Pew Global Stewardship Initiative,[14] who had used that label, named Focus on the Family.[15]

Focus on the Family? Extremist? Absurd as it seems to many Christians, one wonders what it and other pro-life groups have done to earn this distinction? Sure, they support human rights for unborn babies as well as traditional parents. But don't they share the right to express their convictions? Are *all* conservative groups that support the family and the fetus considered extremist? What "rights" does this U.N. conference *really* support? These are important questions, for if freedom is only for those who agree, it's not freedom at all.

The hostility toward Christians and other "extremists" raises questions about some of the hard-won guarantees in the Platform for Action. The following item seems to promise religious freedom, but can we be sure?

> The right to freedom of thought, conscience, and religion is inalienable and must be universally enjoyed. . . . However, it is acknowledged that any form of extremism may have a negative impact on women and can lead to violence and discrimination.[16]

Is religious freedom protected only as long as it isn't labeled "extremist" by those in power? Who will determine what is extremist? Suddenly the promise becomes an ominous threat. Christians and Jews have faced persecution untold times through history for refusing to compromise the truths of the Bible, but American freedom has blotted those memories from our consciousness. Are we once again becoming a minority religion in a hostile culture? We shouldn't be surprised. Remember Jesus said, "If they persecuted Me, they will also persecute you" (John 15:20).

"Women, Religion, and Culture," one of the many seminars on how to fight fundamentalism, labeled Christianity "imperialistic, patriarchal, colonialist, capitalistic, egocentric, racial, and homophobic." The leader of the WCC (World Council of Churches) seminar added, "This is a religion so corrupted I call it religious fundamentalism."[17]

Sadly, many American churches have believed the lies. A Presbyterian (USA) staffer at a workshop sponsored by the WCC claimed that "messages from the Bible, from church tradition, and authorities helped to perpetuate and justify domestic violence, incest, child abuse, and sexual exploitation of girls and women by clergy." She suggested that "any element of Christian tradition that denies the full humanity of women *must be discarded,* ignored, or transformed."[18] (Emphasis added)

Do you see the seeds of persecution?

"If your religious faith was a bit less eclectic and experimental," said Diane Knippers, "you quickly got the impression that you were part of the problem rather than part of the solution."[19] On the other hand, "all types of weird spirituality and invocations of the goddess flourished":

> The irony is that the European Union, once the heart of Christendom, is most recalcitrant in accepting [rights for the family and freedom of religion]. As I sat outside the room where the negotiations were taking place, I watched an

African ambassador erupt at one point. Referring to the Europeans, he asked, "What's wrong with these people? They don't believe in family! They don't believe in religion!"

This is not quite right. They do believe in some kinds of religion. A few days ago, I got a mailing. It said: "What a success! The shrine will travel!" For a suggested donation of $100, one can host the Shrine of the Goddess. . . . The Goddess is coming soon to a location near you.[20]

Decoding Feminist Language

Just where does the family fit in the feminist utopia? The three-word theme of the Beijing conference — equality, development, peace — didn't give a clue. So when Chinese leader Chen Muhua opened the official conference on September 4 with those words, *"Equality, development, and peace* are the common demand,"[21] everyone seemed to agree.

But a different set of goals soon became evident. "There is a massive cover-up of these ideological positions and moral policies that are anti-family and at war against human nature,"[22] said Nancy Schaefer, president and founder of Family Concerns, Inc. She explained:

> Every woman here supports women's economic and political rights. Every woman here supports more opportunities, better education and health, and the stopping of violence and abuse, but these issues are only a smoke screen being used as a front to ultimately promote the radical gender agenda. . . .
>
> The U.S. official delegation, the gender feminist Non-Government Organizations headed by Bella Abzug, and representatives on staff at the U.N. are coordinating a worldwide feminist revolution and cover up.[23]

A new feminist language hid the goals driving the feminist agenda: abolishing male leadership at every level of society and taking control of all issues that affect Western women. The official reasons for the conference dealt with more obvious and global concerns: hunger, illness, drought, and violence. Yet, Western delegates seemed focused on feminist issues such as reproductive rights and sexual orientation. Why?

"We intend to fight like mad for all we want," said Donna Shalala, U.S. Secretary of Health and Human Services. "There is extensive opposition to sexual orientation . . . we have had opposition on other issues . . . but we shall overcome them."[24]

Feminist leaders had planned their offensive long before they came to Beijing. At the "PrepCom" (Preparatory Committee meeting) they discussed the meaning of the word "gender." Mentioned 216 times in the pre-conference Platform for Action adopted at their meeting, it was defined as a "socially constructed" role, not a biological fact. "Gender," they said, "indicates that sex roles and behaviors are artificially constructed and freely chosen."[25]

Do you see how this reasoning fits feminist goals? Lesbians win sympathy for their cause by blaming those "socially constructed" gender roles on male oppression. This frees them to spread their message through public education and increase their number. The larger their number, the greater their political strength. No wonder they fought hard to gain access to the world's children through "gender-sensitive" classroom lessons.

"We will not be forced back to the 'biology is destiny' concept,"[26] thundered Bella Abzug, a "venerable feminist warhorse," as news writer Frederica Mathewes-Green calls her.

Some feminist leaders even wanted to promote "an equality of five genders." They would include "male and female heterosexuals, male and female homosexuals, and

182 · A Twist of Faith

trans or bisexuals."[27] Gone is God's view of gender: "He who made *them* at the beginning 'made them male and female' " (Matt. 19:4).

No one wanted to define the phrase "gender perspective" which was mentioned 45 times in the Platform for Action. When Nancy Schaefer asked the U.S. delegation for a definition, their response was, "We don't define terms!"

"If they don't," asked Nancy later, "how can they possibly expect 186 nations to sign on? Will they bully them into accepting the platform by linking their approval to financial aid?"[28]

The new usage of the term "violence" added to the confusion. It obviously wasn't limited to "the use of physical force so as to damage or injure."[29] What, then, did the Anglican Women's Network mean when they said, "We strive to eliminate economic, political, domestic, cultural, environmental, religious, and sexual violence against women?"

"The network's goal of eliminating violence sounded entirely worthwhile until we read the fine print," said Diane Knippers. "What they are eliminating is any meaningful definition of the word 'violence.' " She gave some examples to show the new usage:

> • *Economic violence* included "unequal distribution of wealth . . . as evidence by world debt" and "no wages for women's work."
> • *Political violence* ranged from genuine examples of violence [such as rape] . . . to "women's exclusion in decision-making."
> • *Religious violence* was "intolerance and persecution of women who will not conform" and "exclusion of women from religious leadership."[30]
> • *Sexual violence* [included] "compulsory heterosexuality."[31]

"In the end, the network's statement deconstructs language and demeans the plight of women who truly suffer violence," concluded Diane Knippers. Rwandan delegate Aloysie Inymba agreed. "I'm here because my people are starving," she said, "and we want to discuss a cure for malaria, not abortions."[32]

Power to Change the World?

Some wonder if the conference will matter in the long run. They cite well-known U.N. problems: shortage of money, lack of consensus, etc. So will Beijing make a difference?

"Yes, enormously," says Diane Knippers, who called it "an arrogant, intrusive, and comprehensive experiment in social engineering."[33] She explained why:

> The Platform for Action adopted in Beijing will be used as a standard for economic, political, and social politics at home and abroad. The Platform will have particular impact in American universities and will be used within the education establishment to determine what our children are taught. Through this conference the values of the Western left will be forced onto other countries.[34]

Actually, the economic, political, and social policies of the platform have *already* been accepted in American universities. In an article, aptly titled "A Road to Hell Paved with Good Intentions," respected economist Thomas Sowell[35] points out that "Marxism as an ideal continues to flourish on American college campuses, as perhaps nowhere else in the world."[36]

Don't underestimate an idea whose time has come. Whether Marxist utopianism or feminist socialism, they spread like cancer when the climate is right. Take the word "gender." Once "safely cordoned off inside the confines of the academy," warns a *Wall Street Journal* editorial, "[it] spread to the courts, government, and Microsoft Word processing program. . . . Lately the PC wisteria has been spotted wrapping itself around elected bodies and international conferences."[37]

According to Donna Shalala, the Clinton White House was committed to carry out the Beijing Platform. As a starter, it would open an "Office of Women's Outreach and Initiatives" which would direct a year-long process that would "involve every federal agency in carrying out the platform." That's a big first step toward acceptance!

Alan Wisdom, vice president of the Institute on Religion and Democracy, is right when he says, "We must re-examine the common assumption that the platform is just another bloated, meaningless effusion of U.N. rhetoric. The American public may be surprised and dismayed when it sees a whole new raft of intrusive, expensive federal programs coming down the river."[38]

Some of those intrusive federal programs have already been put in place through the new education system. Its favorite slogan fits right into the Beijing declaration: "It takes a whole village to raise a child"— the theme of Hillary Clinton's book. Both hide a warning that parents may be forced to share their God-given right to "train up a child in the way he should go"[39] with schools, counselors, psychologists, and health workers determined to teach a contrary set of values.

"Little by little, children are losing their families, and the government is becoming a surrogate parent,"[40] wrote Nancy Schaefer.

The Beijing declaration did finally consent to call the family "the basic unit of society."[41] But the same paragraph also warns us about coming restrictions: "The upbringing of children requires shared responsibility of parents, women and men and society as a whole." It adds a reminder that a woman's role is changing: "Maternity, motherhood, parenting . . . must not . . . restrict the full participation of women in society." Are they implying that women must join the workforce to fulfill the 50/50 workplace quotas?

But, some will protest, didn't the Beijing Declaration promise "freedom of thought, conscience, religion, and belief?" Yes, it did, but remember the reservation: "any form of extremism may have a negative impact on women and can lead to violence and discrimination."[42] That sounds like a wise precaution, but it can also be used against all who oppose the feminist agenda. The key is: who will define "extremism"? Will people be free to follow their conscience and choose their religion — as long as they don't choose the radical feminist view of "extremism": resisting the new social values?

Like the U.S. education system, the platform would require adults as well as children to be trained, re-trained, and remediated through "gender sensitive"[43] courses to make sure they pass the new social standards for acceptance into the global workforce. Its education agenda seems to be an extension of the World Conference on Education for All (WCEFA),[44] the international system which shares the same six basic goals and global agenda as the U.S. education system.

I know this sounds complex. If I tried to summarize the psychological manipulation, politically correct requirements, attitudinal tests, and lifetime surveillance that comes with this global education network, you probably wouldn't believe me. Instead, I suggest that you read my book, *Brave New Schools*,[45] and see for yourself. It will show you that the Beijing agenda fits right into the worldwide education network.

"My people are destroyed for lack of knowledge," (Hos. 4:6) said God. Can you hear the grief in His words? If we close our eyes to the danger signals all around, we won't be ready for the challenges ahead. Don't forget, if this global education movement isn't stopped, parents as well as children will be molded to fit the feminist and globalist plan for transformation.

Keep in mind, the clamor for global socialism didn't begin with the feminist movement. Karl Marx and other revolutionaries started it long before women had a public voice. There's reason to believe they are merely using the women's demands to create the right climate for change. In a 1993 speech at the International Development Conference, James P. Grant, past executive director of the United Nations Children's Fund (UNICEF), stated:

> Children and *women can be our Trojan Horse* for attacking the citadel of poverty, for undergirding democracy, dramatically slowing population growth and for accelerating economic development.[46] (Emphasis added)

A Trojan Horse?

Do you remember the Communist Manifesto? It announced a proletarian revolution which would empower the poor by redistributing all wealth. Resources would be shared according to need, everyone would be equal, and justice would reign. Men and women alike would join the socialist workforce, and their children would be trained by the state.

It happened, didn't it? All but the leaders became almost equally poor, and all the children were indoctrinated with an anti-Christian socialist philosophy. Morally and economically, the masses sank to the level of the lowest common denominator.

Did you notice the similarities between the Communist Manifesto and the Beijing Declaration? In Beijing, radical feminists finally won worldwide — though far from unanimous — support for the revolution they have proclaimed for years. Look at the parallels:

> • Both revolutions are rooted in modern social sciences such as psychology and sociology, which help establish the victimhood, blame, and anger needed to fuel the revolution.

• Both emphasize education as the means to social transformation.

• Both use synthesis (a psychological strategy to blend opposing views into new compromise beliefs that fit the goal) as a strategy to establish "consensus."

• Both appeal to the masses by promising equality through Marxist economics.

• Both spread hatred toward any "extremist belief" that refuses to compromise and affirm *their* "consensus."

• Both lead to religious, moral, and economic bankruptcy.

As you saw earlier, the Platform for Action reshuffles job "opportunities" for both men and women. Employers would have to demonstrate 50/50 gender equality by hiring as many women as men, especially at leadership levels, in all areas: the media, education, industry, politics, etc. "One imagines women dragged away from nursing babies in order to serve on village councils, whether they want to or not,"[47] said reporter Frederica Mathewes-Green.

Which women would run for top political, educational, and media positions — the leading platforms for changing culture? Probably more feminists with politically correct values than women with traditional values. If radical feminists win their 50/50 representation in government, how many would represent *your* values?

Would Jane Fonda? Billed as "a good-will ambassador" of the U.N. on a Chinese television show, she affirmed China's coercive abortion and one-child policy. "All countries should understand what China understands about population control," she said. "I am embarrassed that my own country does not have an official program."[48]

How would employers meet the 50/50 quota if some women choose not to enter the workforce? It's hard to say. Would men be dismissed and forced to work at home? They may — as a drastic means to reverse old trends and traditions.

The Platform for Action indicates that all parents would have to model equality at home.[49] If they don't, they could face remediation[50] (the social retraining or psychological indoctrination programs already being implemented through the new education system). If they refuse to reject the old "sexist" roles, they would surely face punitive measures — perhaps special taxes or loss of social privileges such as drivers licenses or jobs.[51]

A new international surveillance system[52] would ensure that traditional family roles are eradicated and all economic activity tracked and recorded.[53] Operating through nations or regions but controlled by the United Nations,[54] the personalized data files would expose families that refuse to follow feminists guidelines. Women would be assessed for "unremunerated work" — housework, child care, helping others, community service, etc.[55] What does that mean?

"Each family would be given a 'dependency ratio,' " says Joan Veon. "As part of the economic filling for the global cake, it shows whether or not a household is producing enough to warrant its existence." Under the guise of "gender analysis statistics," it would:

> . . . measure how people spend their leisure time and the [number of hours they spend] caring for dependents and working for family businesses, etc. When you [link this kind of surveillance to the regulations needed for] "sustainable development" — which says the world has too many people and the U.N. must be the caretaker of the earth's resources — you get the Marxist-Leninist philosophy of measuring "who is producing and who is consuming the earth's resources . . . all under the guise of 'women's issues."[56]

"By using women as the 'Trojan Horse,' " explained

Joan Veon, "the United Nations would overrule national laws and conform the economics of each country to the concept of 'sustainable development.' Everyone would be assessed both for their economic value and their burden to the global economy. If fully implemented, this program would classify every person according to how much they produce and consume[57] of planetary resources."[58]

That sounds good or scary, depending on where you stand. If you have believed the doomsday scenarios painted by politically correct environmentalists, you will probably agree that the planet already houses more people than it can sustain. On the other hand, if you have read the scientific facts[59] that expose the sensational and inflated scenarios (ozone "hole" destruction, global warming, melting ice caps, etc.) and outrageous doomsday predictions, you may shudder at the prospect of letting environmental "experts" and globalist politicians set the limits on available resources — and the number of people allowed to live and use them.

Falsifying the Evidence

Let me assure you of two important facts. First, the world is full of genuine and devastating environmental problems. Most have to do with local pollution, deforestation, or depletion of ocean life. They usually require local solutions, so they fail to stir enough public indignation to kindle global outrage. Yet, they affect millions of people on marginal incomes, destroy vital habitats and farm land, and get far less media attention than they deserve.

Second, unless God allows the kinds of droughts and floods that devastated Israel when His people turned to other gods, we are not about to run out of food. Under normal conditions, we can raise far more than globalists want us to believe.[60] The main obstacle to feeding hungry masses is distribution, and nothing will harm well-meaning efforts to preserve perishable food more than the horrendous ozone hoax which persuaded nations around the world to sign the

Montreal Protocol banning CFC — the basic coolant in refrigerators.

You see, the green movement is another Trojan horse, and it works hand-in-hand with the worldwide feminist movement. It was formed on college campuses in the sixties by four counter-culture groups: radical feminists, Marxists (the new left), peace-niks (the anti-war movement), and hippies seeking spiritual enlightenment. Then as now, their common enemies were Western culture and Christian values.

Since then, they have learned to win support for planetary management by raising consciousness — a skill fine-tuned by feminist revolutionaries. With the media on their side, they don't even need a *real* global crisis to build awareness and prompt action. They just need believable stories. What counts is *perception,* not facts. As Stanford climate modeler Stephen Schneider points out,

> We need to get some broad-based support to capture the public's imagination. That, of course, entails getting loads of media coverage. So we have to offer up scary scenarios, make simplified, dramatic statements and make little mention of any doubts we might have. . . . Each of us has to decide what the right balance is between being effective and being honest.[61]

Al Gore described just the right "scary scenario" at the 1992 United Nations World Conference on Environment and Development (UNCED) in Rio de Janeiro: "An enormous hole is opening in the ozone layer," he said, "[and] huge quantities of carbon dioxide, methane, and chlorofluorocarbons are trapping heat in the atmosphere and raising global temperatures."[62]

"But isn't that true?" you might ask.

No, it's not.

In a chapter on environmental education in *Brave New*

Schools, I describe and document the environmental hoax and its political purpose. You can find some of the information relating to the mythical ozone "hole" in the endnotes.[63] Honest and respected scientists who are not intimidated by government threats to cut their research grants, are appalled at the politicized reports that are replacing genuine science. They know well that the United Nations and many U.S. politicians are far more devoted to political ideologies than to scientific realities. Dr. Frederick Seitz, past president of the National Academy of Sciences and recipient of the National Medal of Science exposed one of their attempts to deceive the public:

> The Intergovernmental Panel on Climate Change, a U.N. organization regarded by many as the best source of scientific information about the human impact on the earth's climate, released *The Science of Climate Change 1995.* . . . I have never witnessed a more disturbing corruption of the peer review proces. . . . More than 15 sections . . . were changed or deleted after the scientists charged with examining this question had accepted the supposedly final text. . . . The following passages are examples of those deleted:
>
> > None of the studies cited above has shown clear evidence that we can attribute the observed climate changes to . . . increases in greenhouse gases.
> >
> > No study to date has positively attributed all or part of the climate change to . . . man-made causes.
>
> IPCC reports are often called the "consensus" view. If they lead to carbon taxes and restraints on economic growth, they will have a major and almost certainly destructive impact on the economies of the world. . . . Their effect is to

deceive policymakers and the public into believing that the scientific evidence shows human activities are causing global warming.[64]

Would *you* want U.N. ideologies to dictate how you should live?

Trusting the "advice" given by politicized environmentalists would mean slashing the world population so drastically that only the families of elite decision-makers would be safe from unthinkable controls. Remember Sam Keen's statement at the State of the World Forum (chapter 7): "The ecological crisis, in short, is the population crisis. Cut the population by 90 percent and there aren't enough people left to do a great deal of ecological damage."

How do you cut the world's population even by 50 percent? Who would be allowed to bear children? How will those children be controlled? Since China's boarding school programs and one-child-per-family policy has been promoted as models both for U.S. education and sustainable development, I wonder what kinds of repression might be used in the name of sustainability, equality, and peace.

Two things seems certain. First, radical feminists and male globalists are plotting a worldwide social revolution cloaked as concern for the oppressed. Second, they share a common hatred for God and His truth.[65]

God's Power and Glory

"Why do the nations rage, and the people plot a vain thing?" asked the Psalmist. "The kings of the earth set themselves, and the rulers take counsel together, against the Lord and His anointed, saying, 'Let us break their bonds in pieces and cast away their cords from us' " (Ps. 2:1-3).

Can you believe those words were written more than 2,000 years ago? It sounds just like our times. Then as now, the leaders joined together to plot the death of God. They would destroy His influence, break free from His natural order, and establish a new nation — one built according to their own imagination. History shows the devastating results.

But God continues to reign! No matter how much people shun, mock, or slander Him, He remains God. *We*, not He, become the losers when we ignore Him and shun His truth.

"He who sits in the heavens shall laugh," continued the Psalmist. He didn't mean that God enjoys the ridiculous human conspiracies that challenge His eternal sovereignty, but there is something laughable about the utter foolishness of people who fight their own Maker. Who do they think they are?

Mere humans can never stop God's plans any more than two toddlers can plot to take over their city. They can build block towers, toss little action figures, maybe even break a window or two — but they can't control anything. God reigns, whether we trust Him or not.

"The Lord brings the counsel of the nations to nothing, He makes the plans of the peoples of no effect," wrote the author of Psalm 33. "The counsel of the Lord stands forever." To those who know His wisdom, that's good news!

The bad news is that most of the world is following false counsel. The last chapter will look at some of the most seductive spiritual substitutes people have ever imagined. You will see why they fit our times — and what the all-powerful King of the universe has promised to do for those who will trust Him.

Endnotes

[1]Robin Morgan, Ed., *Sisterhood is Powerful:* An Anthology of Writings from the Women's Liberation Movement (New York, NY: Vintage Books, 1970), p. 551.

[2]Barbara Marx Hubbard, *The Revelation* (Greenbrae, CA: The Foundation for Conscious Evolution, 1993), p. 91.

[3]Trina Robbins, *Choices: A Pro-Choice Benefit Comic* (San Francisco, CA: Angry Isis Press, 1990), p. 20.

[4] Diane Knippers, "Building a Shrine in Beijing," *Heterodoxy*, October 19, 1995), p. 7.

[5] The Institute on religion and Democracy (IRD) works for the reformation of the U.S. churches' social and political witness. It founded the Ecumenical Coalition on Women and Society, which counters the influence of radical forms of feminism in the church and society (1521 16th Street, N.W., Suite 300, Washington, D.C. 20036).

[6] Knippers, "Building a Shrine in Beijing," p. 7.

[7] "Scan: Whale-song in the Rainforest," *The American Enterprise,* November/December 1995, p. 9.

[8] Diane Knippers, "The Beijing Conference," *Paradigm 2000,* Summer 1995, p. 17.

[9] Nancy Smith and Donna Maxfield, "Spiritual Quest in Beijing," RENEW Women's Network, *Good News,* November/December 1995, p. 35.

[10] Diane Knippers, "Chinese NGO Delegate Confiscates Petitions for Religious Liberty," *Beijing Bulletin*, September 6, 1995.

[11] Paige Comstock Cunningham, "United Nations Agenda for Women Falls Short," *Christianity Today,* October 23, 1995, p. 91.

[12] *Encyclopedia Britannica* (Chicago, IL: William Benton, 1968), Vol. 5, p. 163.

[13] Michael Miller, " 'Extremist' language unnecessary," *Journal Star,* Peoria, IL, August 26, 1995.

[14] According to Michael Miller, the Pew Global Stewardship Initiative is a subsidiary of the liberal Pew Foundation which funds many globalist and educational organizations.

[15] Michael Miller, " 'Extremist' language unnecessary."

[16] Beijing Declaration, #12; Platform for Action, #25.

[17] Knippers, "Building a Shrine in Beijing."

[18] Diane Knippers, "Final Take on Beijing: 'They Just Don't Get It!'" *Beijing Bulletin*, September 12, 1995.

[19] Knippers, "Building a Shrine in Beijing."

[20] Ibid.

[21] Nancy Schaefer's daily report on the United Nations Conference on Women, Beijing, September 5, 1995, p. 1.

[22] Ibid., 4. (Nancy Schaefer's daily report, September 5, 1995), p. 4. Mrs. Schaefer came to Beijing representing both Family Concerns and the Southern Baptist Convention at the NGO forum.

[23] Ibid., p. 4, 6.

[24] Donna Shalala's answer to a question posed by a reporter from the *San Francisco Chronicle*, September 11, 1995. She was referring to item #48 in the Platform for Action. Cited by Nancy Shaefer, p. 12.

[25] Frederica Mathewes-Green, "The gender agenda," 1995 *Religion News Service*, August 22, 1995.

[26]Ibid.

[27]Ibid.

[28]Shaefer, p. 16.

[29]*The New Lexicon Webster's Dictionary* (New York, NY: Lexicon Publications, 1989).

[30]Diane Knippers, *"Power!"* November/December 1995, p. 10.

[31]Ibid.

[32]Paige Comstock Cunningham, "United Nations Agenda for Women Falls Short," *Christianity Today,* October 23, 1995, p. 91.

[33]Diane Knippers, "Coalition will take message of universal rights to Beijing," *The Presbyterian Layman,* July/August 1995, p. 15.

[34]Diane Knippers, "The Beijing Conference," *Paradigm 2000,* Summer '95, p. 17.

[35]Senior Fellow at the Hoover Institution at Stanford University.

[36]Thomas Sowell, "A Road to Hell Paved with Good Intentions," *Forbes,* January 17, 1994, p. 62.

[37]"Gender Confusion," *Wall Street Journal,* August 18, 1995.

[38]Ibid.

[39]Proverbs 22:6.

[40]Shaefer, p. 10.

[41]Platform for Action, #30.

[42]Beijing Declaration, #12; Platform for Action, #25.

[43]Platform for Action, #85(j, m), 197d.

[44]Platform for Action, #72

[45]Berit Kjos, *Brave New Schools* (Eugene, OR: Harvest House Publishers, 1996).

[46]Joan Veon, *Compilation of the Beijing Draft Document Grouped by Perceived or Stated Goals* (Olney, MD: TWG, Inc., 1995), p. i.

[47]Frederica Mathewes-Green.

[48]Diane Knippers, "White House is Keen on Beijing Platform," *Beijing Bulletin*, September 8, 1995.

[49]Platform for Action #167n,181(c-f) 197d.

[50]Platform for Action #84a, 90(a,c), 125k,181(c-f), 194e, 209f.

[51]Platform for Action #181f. Chester Finn, Jr., director of the Educational Excellence Network in Washington D.C., who helped Education Secretary Lamar Alexander write the blueprint for Outcome-Based Education, wrote the following suggestion for enforcing the new global values in education: "Perhaps the best way to enforce this standard is to confer valuable benefits and privileges on people who meet it, and to withhold them from those who do not. Work permits, good jobs, and college admission are the most obvious, but there is ample scope here for imagination in devising carrots and sticks. Drivers' licenses could be deferred. So could eligibility for professional athletic teams. The minimum wage paid to those who

earn their certificates [Certificates of Initial Mastery] might be a dollar higher. . . ." Chester Finn, Jr., *We Must Take Charge: Our Schools and Our Future* (New York, NY: The Free Press, 1991), p. 257.

[52] Platform for Action #70(a,b), 192e, 194(b,g), 195c, 196c, 258b.

[53] Platform for Action #209(a-k), 211a, 212.

[54] Platform for Action #314, 319, 327.

[55] Platform for Action #167g, 209f, 209g.

[56] Joan Veon, *Compilation of the Beijing Draft Document*, p. 6.

[57] Platform for Action #37.

[58] Stated in telephone conversation with Joan Veon, December 7, 1995.

[59] Read Ronald Bailey's *The True State of the Planet:* Ten of the World's Premier Environmental Researchers in a Major Challenge to the Environmental Movement (New York, NY: The Free Press, 1995). Among its respected contributors are Dr. Bruce Ames, professor of biochemistry and molecular biology and director of the National Institute of Environmental Health Sciences Center at the University of California, Berkeley; Roger A. Sedjo, Senior Fellow in the Energy and Natural Resources Division at Resources for the Future and co-author of *The Long-term Adequacy of World Timber Supply*. To order the CFACT environmental newsletter contact CFACT at P.O. Box 65722, Washington, D.C. 20035.

[60] The "normal" weather conditions of the Northern Hemisphere during the 20th century may not be normal for the long run. Both weather and climate undergo cyclical changes based on a long string of factors that influence air currents, ocean currents, magnetic forces, etc. If the climate warms, more ocean water will evaporate, more rain will fall, and more food will be produced. A cooling trend would slow evaporation, dry the land, slow ripening grain, and devastate agriculture around the world.

[61] Jonathan Schell, "Our Fragile Earth," *Discover,* October 1989, p. 44.

[62] Prepared remarks, typescript distributed at the United Nations' Earth Summit in Rio de Janeiro, June 1992.

[63] Actually the ozone "hole" is not a hole at all. It is a seasonal thinning discovered back in 1956 by Dr. Gordon Dobson, explains Dr. Edward Krug, who has degrees in environmental and soil sciences and is listed in *Who's Who in Science and Engineering*. Each spring, after the long sunless southern winter, the ozone layer thins over the Antarctica. Conversely, it *always* expands after the southern summer when ultraviolet radiation once again creates ozone. (The media didn't tell you that the "hole" closes each year, did it?) The annual thinning varies from year to year. In fact, less ozone was measured in 1985 than in 1990 though more freon was used. Why? Scientific data indicate a strong consistent correlation between

ozone depletion and major volcanic explosions and other natural factors.

The cost of the ozone hoax defies comprehension. "The ban on CFC's will cost as much as $5 trillion by 2005," says Dr. Krug. "Eight hundred million refrigerators and freezers will have to be replaced worldwide as non-corrosive CFC's will be replaced by highly expensive and *corrosive* chemicals like HCFC. . . . [This ban will] severely undermine efforts to feed millions in the Third World."

[64]Frederick Seitz, "A Major Deception on Global Warming," *The Wall Street Journal*, 12 June 1996.

[65]Chapter 10 will amplify this assertion. For in-depth documentation and illustrations read my book on the new global education system, *Brave New Schools*. Globalist leaders call for a new set of global beliefs and values in order to create a world without war and conflict. They view Christianity as their greatest hindrance.

Chapter 10

Yours . . . Forever,
or
Nothing Is Permanent?

❧

Religion and culture are ever changing, ever transforming. . . . We are the transformer, maker and creator of our own religious and cultural traditions. ("Women, Religion, and Culture" seminar, Beijing Conference)[1]

Human culture will change in the next millennium as a result of conscious evolution. (James Redfield, *Celestine Prophecy*)[2]

He has put eternity in their hearts. (Eccles. 3:11)

❧

"Do you go to church back home?" I asked Karin in her native Norwegian. The blonde, blue-eyed exchange student was visiting our church, and I had enjoyed catching up on the latest news about Norway. But now it was time to move on to my special assignment.

Since her California host family found it difficult to

communicate with her about spiritual things in English, they had asked me to find out whether she was a Christian or not.

"No," she answered.

"Are there many Christians in your school?"

"There are some who go to church at Christmas or Easter."

"That sounds like me, back when I lived there. We only went to church on Christmas Eve, and no one took it very seriously. But now I am more interested in spiritual things. I keep wondering how people who don't know God face things like cancer and death? Do you ever wonder what will happen to you when you die?

"I'll go to some sort of heaven. I'm a nice person."

"How do you know you're nice enough?"

"I think I am. Most people are."

"Who sets the standard for the niceness needed to get into heaven?"

She shrugged. "I don't know. Probably God."

Sensing both disinterest and annoyance, I quickly brought the conversation back inside the boundaries of her comfort zone.

Did Karin's reasoning sound familiar? It did to me. She admitted that God might set the standards, but she doesn't know Him, so she simply imagines what He wants. In other words, she sets her own standards.

This new-paradigm thinking is changing people everywhere. Karin believes there will be a heaven — not because God says so, but because it comforts her and hides the finality of death. Why throw out a good idea? But her view of heaven is little more than a pie-in-the-sky hope. Like most people today, she has no firm basis for questioning the exciting New Age pieces of the puzzle she calls heaven.

True and false views of heaven	
Judeo-Christian	**Feminist-New Age-Global**
The only door is Jesus Christ	Any "good" faith will do
Without Jesus, I'm not good enough	I am good enough
God reveals His standard for entrance	I choose my standard
We help each other meet His standard	We don't interfere with another's standards
Each person chooses	Humanity evolves together

A New Kind of Heaven

You met Barbara Marx Hubbard, president of the Foundation for Conscious Evolution, in chapter 5. When she spoke at the Renaissance of Christian Spirituality Conference in San Francisco, some of her followers urged me to buy her book *Revelation,* which was dictated by a spirit "voice" called "Christ." I bought it, and shuddered as I read her occult interpretations of God's Book of Revelation. Those who know God's Word would notice its eerie likeness to God's original message. Those who don't know the biblical version could easily think this is *it.*

"Now you see through a glass darkly," wrote Mrs. Hubbard, twisting biblical truth into a confusing mishmash of occult ideas. "Soon you will see face to face. Now you are in pain. Then you will be in joy. Now you fear that you cannot manage a complex planetary system. Soon you will know that the planetary system is guided by a cosmic template. . . . A New Heaven and a New Earth shall you create."

Heaven, she continues, "is but the next stage of your

development, with many more to come."[3]

Since the "voice" first spoke to Barbara Marx Hubbard in 1980, it has taught her about a "collective transformation" that will take place when a "critical mass" of "individuals align to shift the basic thought form of earth from fear and separation to unity" and thus "shift the consciousness of the earth" and lead to a new "birth."[4] If humanity cooperates with the plan, each human "mind will be consciously connected with the mind of God." Those who don't will be "selected" for destruction.[5]

Does this sound too strange to be relevant? It shouldn't. Much of this teaching is seeping into mainstream churches as well as the rest of our culture — not because the masses are listening to Barbara Marx Hubbard, but because her source is the same as theirs. Occultism cloaked in "Christianese" has become part of our common language, challenging us to study God's Word and "test the spirits."

Listen carefully to Mrs. Hubbard's words, for Satan is counterfeiting everything that's good these days — even good things like joy and laughter:

> An uncontrollable joy will ripple through the thinking layer of earth. The co-creative systems, which are lying psychologically dormant in humanity will be activated. From within, all sensitive persons will feel the joy of the force, flooding their systems with love and attraction. It will be as irresistible as sex. It is suprasex, the innate capacity to unite to create the next step of evolution. . . .
>
> As this joy flashes through the nervous systems of the most sensitive peoples on earth, it will . . . cause a shift in the consciousness of earth.[6]

Don't ever fear genuine joy, but be guarded against any uncontrollable manifestation of spiritual power. God calls us to self-control, and forces that take control over our bodies and manipulate our minds are not from Him.[7] And if the "good feelings" that follow spiritual experiences don't line up with Scriptures, beware.

In other words, know the genuine truth well enough to recognize the counterfeits. The lies come in all kinds of wrappings and disguises. You may have heard of Arianna Huffington, one of the fast-rising female stars in conservative political circles and Washington society. The title of her latest book, *The Fourth Instinct,* refers to a spiritual force with "power to transform ourselves and our world." You know she is not talking about God when she calls it "the bridge to this next stage in man's evolution and the voice calling us to cross over."[8]

"Even those who are not looking for 'a new heaven and a new earth' . . . recognize that what the millennium requires from us above all else is a psychological shift, a spiritual breakthrough,"[9] she says. The Fourth Instinct "is an evolutionary spiral based on a different set of imperatives — for now the survival of the fittest will be the survival of the wisest."[10]

The wisest? According to whom?

Not to Christians who are still "clinging to the old"[11] world-view or paradigm which offers only "the bankrupt solutions of yesterday." They know all too well that "the wisdom of this world is foolishness with God," for "The Lord knows the thoughts of the wise, that they are futile" (1 Cor. 3:19-20).

Instead, Ms. Huffington urges her flock to follow a "universal force that will lead us beyond the last horizon of our known self toward a wiser, more loving, more luminous state of being."[12]

That brings us back to Barbara Marx Hubbard. "To be wise now, is to . . . take the evolutionary perspective and see the world in process of transformation," she says. "Wisdom is to see reality, not as a static set of things, but as a . . . process leading toward godhood for humanity."[13]

Strange and mystical, isn't it? So is James Redfield's

top-selling thriller, *The Celestine Prophecy*. Its huge readership proves the appeal of this occult message. Like Mrs. Hubbard and Mrs. Huffington, Redfield urges humanity to practice the psychic skills needed to produce a "critical mass" in order to speed our evolution. That means rejecting church leaders who block the new awareness.

When a local United Methodist church announced a weekly discussion group on *The Celestine Prophecy*, I decided to check it out. On my first visit, I found a group of about 20 men and women sharing their strange "coincidences," angelic visitations,[14] and other mystical experiences which supposedly led to a "conscious evolution"— the focus of Barbara Marx Hubbard's message. Perhaps they believed, as Redfield promised, that they would one day transform into "pure light" and simply "walk into heaven."[15] In spite of the church setting, no one ever mentioned the likely possibility of counterfeit spirits. Apparently, the group viewed *all* kinds of spiritual feelings and experiences as good. Redfield's lie had become more believable than God's truth:

> For half a century now, a new consciousness has been entering the human world, a new awareness that can only be called transcendent, spiritual. . . .
>
> Once we understand . . . how to engage this allusive process and maximize its occurrence in our lives, human society will take a quantum leap into a whole new way of life. . . .
>
> All that any of us have to do is suspend our doubts and distractions just long enough . . . and miraculously, this reality can be our own.[16]

During the last Celestine Prophecy session, the teacher told us that we were close to becoming the "critical mass" of evolving minds that would catapult us into the next stage of "our" spiritual evolution. There we would accelerate the pace of our evolution and voluntarily limit reproduction and consumption. "Whole groups of people who have reached a certain level [would] become invisible, and the barrier between this life and the other world" would begin to crumble.

"Would we still have criminals?" asked a woman.

"There would be no need to steal, for all have the same values," answered the teacher. "We're moving toward heaven, a state of being where people are valued for their essence. . . . Fundamentalist people live . . . in a state of fear. . . . But someone who is truly spiritual, is serene. She lives in a state of grace."

"My sister-in law is like that," said another women. "She is wonderful. Always in that state of serenity, even when things get really hard."

"What does she believe?" asked the leader.

"In God. In Jesus Christ. She hurts a lot, but she has perfect peace."

The leader changed the subject.

The Sin of Separation

Did you ever read Aldous Huxley's futuristic classic, *Brave New World*? If you did, you may remember the occult ritual used to enforce planetary peace and oneness. No one could escape the hypnotic drills that quenched individualism and raised group consciousness: "The group was now complete, the solidarity circle perfect . . . Twelve of them ready to be made one, waiting to come together, to be fused, to lose their 12 separate identities in a larger being."[17]

Huxley's *Brave New World* carried a warning that few have taken seriously. Today many of its scary ideas are more pervasive than when Huxley first suggested them — not because his voice sang louder than others, but because so many others sang in the same choir. Since their message fit both current trends and academic liberalism, it began to resonate through our educational institutions at every level.

Today, it's preparing a new generation for social revolution, and radical feminists want girls to lead the way.

United Nations leader Robert Muller may not care which sex leads the revolution as long as Huxley's unity becomes global reality. "Conflicts will diminish as our global, universal, spiritual, and cosmic awareness increase,"[18] he assures us. Ripe for change, many are listening. The fact that Muller's mystical unity matches the spiritual evolution taught by Barbara Marx Hubbard, Arianna Huffington, and James Redfield multiplies the influence of all four.

Muller is no small player in the global transformation. As the former undersecretary of the United Nations and the current chancellor of the UN-sponsored University of Peace, he may be the world's most enthusiastic promoter of the kind of international education system outlined by the radical feminists in Beijing. His World Core Curriculum, which laid the foundation for global education in the United States and around the world, is based on the messages received from the Tibetan Master Djwhal Khul, the spirit guide channeled by occultist Alice Bailey.

Does all this seem complicated? It *is*. I wish we could ignore these lies and occult networks. We probably could, if they weren't already transforming our churches. But since they have twisted the way Christians see God, heaven, and everything else, we can't ignore them. Too many people are falling into the trap.

Another window into the widening web of globalism opened at the 1994 "Women of Vision" Conference in Washington, D.C. The highlight of the event was the World Peace Ceremony which joined the audience of 500 women and 50 men in a universal prayer for peace. Many had tears in their eyes as they prayed to a cosmic force, not God, for universal love and forgiveness.[19]

Among the guests at the conference were Barbara Marx Hubbard, the Dalai Lama's sister Jetsun Pema, and Ann Rockefeller Roberts, president of the Fund of the Four

Directions (remember all those sacred circles that honored the four directions) which helps wed the Rockefeller fortune to New Age globalism and Native American spirituality.

Robert Muller was there as well. Do you see the many mystical marriages that will help usher in the new global society — the counterfeit heaven on earth? The "Mind" behind the new global spirituality sends the same basic messages to all his ambassadors, whether they call themselves New Agers, neo-pagans, or even "Christian."

The connections are important, because no single group could win the world to these new ideals. That radical feminists like Bella Abzug claim the right to speak for *all* the women in the world may seem absurd, but so what? She, Muller, Hubbard, and all the rest are each playing their part in the globalist orchestra determined to raise global consciousness and speed the paradigm shift. They may be strangers to each other, but the evil puppeteer behind the scenes knows how to pull the strings and guide the action. That's what counts. Few realize that the angry idealism of feminist activists can be used by hard-core globalist to reach a more ominous goal. As economist Dr. Thomas Sowell wrote in his review of *Road to Serfdom,*

> Idealist socialists create systems in which *idealists are almost certain to lose* and be superseded by those whose drive for power, and ruthlessness in achieving it, make them the "fittest" to survive under a system where government power is the ultimate prize. . . . The issue is not what anyone intends but what consequences are in fact likely to follow.[20]

In other words, idealists can persuade, but they seldom rule. Idealism can awaken the masses and inspire a revolution, but it seldom governs. During the first part of the Russian revolution, ideology paved the way to change. But the manipulative power of Communist forces soon seized the victory and captured the throne.

Like the radical feminists at the Beijing Conference, Muller and other U.N. leaders have no tolerance for non-conformists. When speaking at some of the 1995 events celebrating the 50th anniversary of the United Nations, Muller shared his vision for the future: a united world where all would live in harmony sharing a common set of global values. People were free to believe anything — as long as it was pantheistic, monistic, and polytheistic. Even cross-less Christianity would fit. Biblical faith would not.

He told us how to reach this utopia. The world would need "a global ethic" — a common set of beliefs, values, and behavior. These would be universally enforced — yes, in the USA as well as in the rest of the world. A new World Court would be given power and authority "to condemn" wrong behavior and prosecute violators.

What kinds of legal standards would guide humans in their pursuit of peace? Muller listed some of them. The new laws would deal with the problems of over-population, over-consumption, garbage, business, and religious differences. "The next millennium must heal what is wrong," he concluded. Those "wrongs" included free enterprise, biblical Christianity, large families, and freedom to dissent. Do they remind you of the Beijing Platform for Action? (See chapter 9.)

When the moderator invited questions from the audience, a man stood up. The startling exchange that followed left me with an uneasy insight into a form of intolerance that is incomprehensible to most Americans. The man's two questions seemed thoughtful and legitimate by traditional Western standards. Wouldn't you agree? He asked:

> In a pluralistic world, would a centralized institution tend to become insensitive to ideas other than its own? And if the U.N. becomes involved in spirituality, could it cause church-state violations?

In response, an angry woman in the audience stood up and shouted, "In Oklahoma we saw the result of men who hate our central government." She stormed out of the auditorium.

Sounding just as angry, Muller leaned into the microphone and began denouncing both people and nations who oppose global controls. After venting his anger on the USA for its reluctance to show wholehearted support for U.N. policies, he swore and left the podium. Is this the kind of tolerance the U.N. touts? Could Muller be so accustomed to approval from like-minded globalists, that he can tolerate nothing less?

Persecution

Muller's hatred for those who disagree permeates the movement toward a global spirituality. It doesn't matter whether the individual links are called witchcraft, feminist spirituality, Native American shamanism, or simply global spirituality. All envision a world where all human minds are connected to some kind of a global mind — call it the goddess as Wiccans do, the "collective unconscious" as Carl Jung did, "unity consciousness" as does "Christian theologian" John Bradshaw, or the "Mind of God" as does Barbara Marx Hubbard.

Since all versions of spiritual globalism follow the same occult master, they share a common hatred for the biblical God and His truth. "The world . . . hates Me because I testify of it that its works are evil," said Jesus (John 7:7). It hates us, for the same reason. Therefore, opposition to the cosmic plan can be costly. As Barbara Marx Hubbard warns us, "The selection process will exclude all who are exclusive. The selection process assures that only the loving will evolve to the stage of co-creator."[21]

Those who are "loving" in Ms. Hubbard's eyes will be linked to the cosmic "Mind" she follows, and *it* will inspire their attitudes and actions. Genuine Christians would be "selected" out of Hubbard's evolutionary scheme. It sounds like a scary fantasy, but it comes close to what God told us would happen.

"Then they will deliver you up to tribulation and kill you," said Jesus, "and you will be hated by all nations for My name's sake" (Matt. 24:9). Remove the phrase "all nations," and He could have been referring to almost any time during the last two thousand years. Long ago, Roman Christians fought lions. Missionaries to Asia, Africa, and South America were tortured, burned, and stabbed. Untold millions were tormented and killed by Communists who rejected Christ but not impersonal psychic powers. And Nazi resistors faced the gas chambers along with the millions of Jews.

For two centuries the spreading influence of Christianity calmed the seething hostilities of occultism, and God's people found a momentary haven. But our shelter may soon be ravaged by the coming millennial storms. "Many will be offended, will betray one another, and will hate one another," continued Jesus. "Then many false prophets will rise up and deceive many. And because lawlessness will abound, the love of many will grow cold. But he who endures to the end shall be saved" (Matt. 24:10-13).

Endure? Where does endurance fit into the American dream? Or into contemporary church teaching? Or the feminist movement?

Endurance is one of the forgotten virtues, isn't it? Yet it's crucial to the battles ahead, whether end times are near us or still far away. Either way, it's time to prepare for radical changes. For the biblical and historical pattern shows us that when God's people or nations ignored truth, returned to paganism, and worshiped other gods, everyone suffered. With a heart that ached over the pain of His people (Jer. 8:9-9:1), God would pull back His hand of protection[22] and allow His people to face the terrors of life without Him — usually droughts, famines, wars, and plagues.

Eventually, the people would see what life was like without the Shepherd. The priests would roll out the dusty old Scriptures, tear their clothes in despair of their own rebellion, repent, and pray for healing. God always forgave and restored, for then as now He wants nothing more than to bless His precious people.

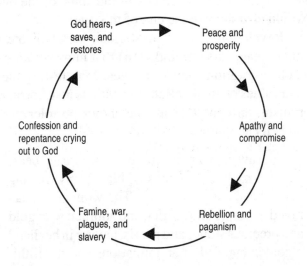

In spite of the glaring similarities between ancient Israel and today, there are some sobering differences. The vast communication network for occult indoctrination, the proliferation of seductive spiritual counterfeits, and our ignorance of occult dangers have set the stage for potential occult dominance that knows no precedent. In light of biblical prophecy, could the oft-repeated cycle have become a downward spiral?

I don't know. God hasn't told us His schedule. Jesus gave us some signs to look for, but not the starting date for the tyrannical world government prophesied in Revelation 13. Only one thing is certain. The dreaded reign of the final Antichrist[23] will come, but it will last only a moment in time.

"Learn this parable from the fig tree," said Jesus after

telling His disciples about the false prophets, lawlessness, apostasy, and persecution that would characterize the last days. "When its branch . . . puts forth leaves, you know that summer is near. So you also, when you see all these things, know that it is near, at the very doors" (Matt. 24:32-33).

Years later, Jesus appeared in visions to his beloved disciple John. Now, glorious and awesome as the mighty Heavenly King, He showed His friend some of the events that would characterize the end of this age.

In Revelation 17, the mysterious harlot of the Old Testament reappears, reminding us that human nature and its occult inspirations never changes. Manifesting the beliefs and values of ancient Babylon with its lust, corruption, materialism, and polytheism, she shows no tolerance for God and His people:

> I saw a woman sitting on a scarlet beast *which was* full of names of blasphemy, having seven heads and ten horns. The woman was arrayed in purple and scarlet, and adorned with gold and precious stones and pearls, having in her hand a golden cup full of abominations and the filthiness of her fornication. And on her forehead a name *was* written: MYSTERY, BABYLON THE GREAT, THE MOTHER OF HARLOTS AND OF THE ABOMINATIONS OF THE EARTH. I saw the woman, drunk with the blood of the saints and with the blood of the martyrs of Jesus (Rev. 17:3-6).

Mystery Babylon rides into global prominence on the back of the "beast" which represents the final world government. This reign of tyranny slaughters the Babylonian prostitute:

> Then he said to me, "The waters which you saw, where the harlot sits, are peoples, multitudes,

nations, and tongues. And the ten horns which you saw on the beast, these will hate the harlot, make her desolate and naked, eat her flesh and burn her with fire. For God has put it into their hearts to fulfill His purpose, to be of one mind, and to give their kingdom to the beast, until the words of God are fulfilled (Rev. 17:15-17).

Why would the beast want to destroy the whore? Won't they both follow the same global "Mind" and its demonic hordes?

Yes, but at the end, they seem to part company. The self-determination, rebellion, and polytheism which characterizes neo-paganism serves the purpose of turning people from Christianity to paganism, but they won't fit Satan's final totalitarian plans. His reign may not last long, but while it does, the global tyrant will demand absolute allegiance from *all* his subjects. Each must worship him or die. He will tolerate neither the individualism nor the "other gods" that characterize today's feminist/neo-pagan movement. But the brunt of his fury will be aimed at those who love God:

And all the world marveled and followed the beast. . . . Then he opened his mouth in blasphemy against God, to blaspheme His name, His tabernacle, and those who dwell in heaven. It was granted to him to make war with the saints and to overcome them. And authority was given him over every tribe, tongue, and nation. All who dwell on the earth will worship him, whose names have not been written in the Book of Life of the Lamb slain from the foundation of the world. . . . (Rev. 13:3, 6-8).

Only God knows when these last steps will become reality, but He urges us to heed the warnings. "Blessed is the one who reads the words of this prophecy," wrote the apostle John in his introduction to his end-time visions, "and blessed are those who hear it and take to heart what is written in it" (Rev. 1:3).

It's easier to focus on daily needs than to look at eternal things. But God tells us to be alert and ready, not distracted from His concerns. "As the days of Noah *were,* so also will the coming of the Son of Man be," said Jesus. "For as in the days before the flood, they were eating and drinking, marrying and giving in marriage, until the day that Noah entered the ark, and did not know until the flood came and took them all away, so also will the coming of the Son of Man be. . . . Watch therefore" (Matt. 24:36-42).

One day — perhaps very soon — Jesus will come for His people. We will meet Him in the air, be transformed in His wonderful presence, and be saved from the final terrors of a world that worships evil.

But the Bible offers no guarantee that this glorious event will precede the kind of persecution that countless Christians around the world have endured ever since Jesus was mocked and killed. A new tide of hatred and persecution is rising in America, calling us to a deeper understanding of what it means to suffer, endure, hope, and persevere — ever watching and waiting for the return of the King who died for us.

The first lesson in watchfulness is to know and love truth. Satan will use all kinds of exciting miracles to prove his divine power, and most people will believe his boasts. For "the coming of the lawless one will be in accordance with the work of Satan displayed in all kinds of counterfeit miracles, signs, and wonders, and in every sort of evil that deceives those who are perishing. *They perish because they refused to love the truth*" (2 Thess. 2:9). Pray this will not happen to those you love!

The second lesson follows. Since those who love truth will be hated by the world, we need to fix our eyes on the eternal life that no one can ever take from us. A story I heard long ago shows the joy that comes with a heavenly focus. I don't remember the exact words, but the story goes something like this.

Back in the second century, Roman authorities told the Christian leader Polycarp to stop warning people about paganism and cease telling them the life-saving truth about Jesus Christ. He refused.

"Then we'll take all your possessions," they told him.

"Go ahead," he said. "My God has promised to supply all I need according to His riches in glory. He will take care of me" (Phil. 4:17-19).

"If you don't stop preaching, we'll take your wife and children and kill them," they threatened.

"You can't kill them," he answered, "for they belong to God. I will spend all eternity in heaven with them."

"Then we'll kill you."

"That would be best of all, for I would go immediately into the presence of my Lord. Nothing could be more wonderful."

To us who now look back into history, Polycarp's cruel martyrdom magnifies the joy of his eternal perspective. His faith lives on as a wonderful reminder that when we are joined to Christ through the Cross, we have an eternal treasure in heaven. This assurance doesn't diminish our present life; it makes it richer and fuller. "For to me, to live *is* Christ, and to die *is* gain," said Paul. Living or dying, he enjoyed the privileges of citizenship in heaven. Either way he would serve the God he loved. Death would have been easier, for while he lived, he was stoned, imprisoned, chained, tortured, starved, and beaten for his faith. Yet, he radiated hope:

> Therefore we do not lose heart. Even though our outward man is perishing, yet the inward *man* is being renewed day by day. For our light affliction, which is but for a moment, is working for us a far more exceeding *and* eternal weight of glory,

while we do not look at the things which are seen,
but at the things which are not seen. For the things
which are seen *are* temporary, but the things
which are not seen *are* eternal (2 Cor. 4:16-18).

Heaven Is Forever

What unseen things did Paul "see"? What thoughts
comforted him when His body ached, his food was gone, and
his friends forsook him?

Friends and food may be important, but they meant
little compared to "the excellence of the knowledge of
Christ Jesus my Lord" (Col. 3:1-3). Nothing weakened his
confidence that "the sufferings of this present time are not
worthy *to be compared* with the glory which shall be
revealed in us" (Rom. 8:18). Part of that glory would be a
whole new beautiful body in place of the old broken one:

> *The body* is sown in corruption, it is raised in
> incorruption. . . . It is sown a natural body, it is
> raised a spiritual body. . . . Behold, I tell you a
> mystery: We shall not all sleep, but we shall all be
> changed — in a moment, in the twinkling of an
> eye, at the last trumpet. . . . Death is swallowed up
> in victory. O Death, where *is* your sting? (1 Cor.
> 15:42-55).

All pain and tears would be wiped away. "He will
swallow up death forever," wrote Isaiah, "and the Lord God
will wipe away tears from all faces" (Isa. 25:8). Instead of
pain and loss, there would be an inheritance — something so
wonderful and glorious that we can't even comprehend it
with our present earth-bound minds. Paul saw only a glimpse,
but we can sense his anticipation:

> The Spirit Himself bears witness with our
> spirit that we are children of God, and if children,
> then heirs — heirs of God and joint heirs with

Christ, if indeed we suffer with *Him,* that we may
also be glorified together (Rom. 8:16-17).

Special blessings would be reserved for those who
suffer for His sake.[24] Among the first in line would be those
who gave their lives to do His will, but received little or no
human praise for their faithfulness. In heaven, their "Father
who sees in secret will reward" them with a love that far
exceeds our finite understanding.[25]

While God, in His perfect justice, promises special
rewards for those who gave Him their lives, all of heaven's
citizens will find their "cup" of happiness overflowing. This
final joy will be far deeper and fuller than all the earthly
delights combined. Lacking earthly words for heavenly
glories, the Bible can only use inadequate images like
mansions and streets of gold to symbolize the very best the
human mind can communicate. But those barely hint at the
wonder and magnificence of our future home. "For now we
see in a mirror, dimly (1 Cor. 13:12).

Yet, by faith we can count on God's matchless creativity. He who designed the majestic redwood tree, the multicolored orchid, the royal lion, and the iridescent butterfly for
this finite planet will surely add to His new earth (Rev. 21:1)
a dimension of beauty and splendor that we can't even
conceive. When He delivers His creation "from the bondage
of corruption into the glorious liberty of the children of
God," we will gaze in awe and delight with joy unspeakable
at the brilliance of all He has prepared for us (Rom. 8:21).

New bodies, a new earth, no more pain, a heavenly
inheritance that will last forever. . . . While those promises
delight my heart, they can't compare with the best of all:
meeting our Bridegroom "face to face." We will stand
before a wonderfully real person, the King of the universe —
not simply an impersonal "glory" or radiating "light" as
some tell us. Many saints have described that heavenly
moment, but no earthly words can do it justice. Paul tried:

"Then we who are alive *and* remain shall be caught up together with them in the clouds to meet the Lord in the air," he rejoiced, "and thus we shall always be with the Lord" (1 Thess. 4:17).

Do you see the contrast between the evolutionary one-world spirituality and the unchanging heavenly realm? Unlike the new paradigm with its evolving human consciousness that absorbs human identity, the biblical truth is that we individually will spend eternity in the presence of Jesus Christ, who "is the same yesterday, today and forever" (Heb. 13:8).

Jesus' beloved friend and disciple John sensed how the wonder of God's eternal nature would touch our human lives in that moment of transformation: "Beloved, now we are children of God," he began, "and it has not yet been revealed what we shall be, but we know that when He is revealed, we shall be like Him, for we shall see Him as He is." Then he nudges us to take hold of this magnificent hope and keep it as a banner in our hearts: "And everyone who has this hope in Him purifies himself, just as He is pure" (1 John 3:1-3).

This hope changes us even now. Almost imperceptibly, a new understanding — a more perfect and heavenly paradigm — begins to guide our hearts. "We can't feel at home in this world any more," goes an old song, for we realize that "our citizenship is in heaven!" (Phil. 3:19-20). Like the heroes and heroines of God's hall of fame (Heb. 11), we fix our eyes on the heavenly city that beckons to all God's sojourners. The eyes of our hearts turn to Jesus, "and the things of earth grow strangely dim."

"We don't 'fit' here. It's not our environment!" writes the beloved author and artist Joni Eareckson Tada in her wonder-filled book *Heaven*.[26] Demonstrating the joy of Jesus from her wheelchair, she opens a welcome window into eternal realities.

"Face to face with Christ my Savior," sang Fanny

Crosby, the blind hymnwriter who saw eternal realities more clearly than most people with eyes that see. Her songs still encourage thousands of believers to walk with God all the way home:

> All the way my Savior leads me,
>> What have I to ask beside?
> Can I doubt His tender mercy,
>> Who through life has been my Guide?
> Heavenly peace, divinest comfort,
>> Here by faith in Him to dwell!
> For I know, whate'er befall me,
>> Jesus doeth all things well.
>
> All the way my Savior leads me;
>> Cheers each winding path I tread.
> Gives me grace for every trial,
>> Feeds me with the living bread.
> Though my weary steps may falter,
>> And my soul athirst may be,
> Gushing from the Rock before me,
>> Lo, a spring of joy I see!
>
> All the way my Savior leads me;
>> O the fullness of His love!
> Perfect rest to me is promised
>> In my Father's house above.
> When my spirit clothed immortal,
>> Wings its flight to realms of day,
> This my song through endless ages:
>> Jesus led me all the way!

The Journey Home

The way to heaven is never smooth for those who love God. It means suffering those "needs, persecutions, and distresses" that train us to trust, persevere, and triumph (2

Cor. 12:9-10). It means clinging to God's Word while the world twists His eternal truths into every kind of deception the human mind can invent and demonic forces can inspire.

It means letting God use our weaknesses, not our strengths, to demonstrate His sufficiency along our winding journey (1 Cor. 1:18-28). The best of our own strength can neither fulfill God's purposes nor bring us into heaven. This simple fact offends women like Karin who imagine their own standards for God's approval. "The cross is foolishness" to those who would boast of their own performance rather than God's perfections — and would trade our Father's heaven for a goddess-powered earth. A Lutheran friend, Jane Larson, summarized it well:

> The one true God is He who died on a cross as a condemned felon to save us miserable sinners. This isn't an image that flatters men or women. It may offend anti-Semites that He was a Jew. It may offend feminists that he was male and invited us to pray in His name to God as our Father. God came to us at a particular time and place in a particular person.
>
> This particularity is offensive to those who want to re-image God in their own image. As Lutheran Seminary professor Diane Jacobson has said approvingly, "Many people want and crave a female aspect to divinity." So what else is new?
>
> Long ago, God's people wanted a golden calf. Leaders rose up to give to them. There will always be cravings for self-glorification. There will always be false shepherds and false shepherdesses who will accommodate such cravings.[27]

While He walked on earth, Jesus Christ was a flesh-and-blood human being, not a mythical god formed by the human imagination. He *was* and *is* God who, for a moment in time, left the unseen eternal to enter into human history.

His life, suffering, and death were documented historical facts, not fables told by creative storytellers. What He told us about humility, death, and resurrection is not open to our re-interpretation. "If we, or an angel from heaven, preach any other gospel to you than what we have preached to you, let him be accursed," wrote Paul (Gal. 1:1-24).

On the other hand, if we will come to Him in our need and let His Word like a beacon guide us through the times ahead, He will prove His faithfulness over and over and over. One simple way to come close to Him, is simply to follow the prayer outline Jesus taught His disciples long ago.

In New Testament times, rabbis often provided index-prayers or patterns for prayer. Each short part suggested needs that God's people could amplify. The Lord's prayer (Matt. 6:9-13) can do that and far more, if we will use it as a pathway to intimacy with God. When we do, He opens our eyes to see from His perspective, enables us to share His heart, and keeps us close to himself as we continue our earthly journey:

1. *"Our Father in heaven, holy is Your Name." WORSHIP HIM!* Whether by inner acknowledgment or outward motion, bow before the King, your Father and Shepherd, in faith, love, humility, and surrender, the attitude of worship. Whisper or speak His names (Jesus, Shepherd, Father, Abba, King, Prince of Peace, El Shaddai, Bridegroom . . .), letting them remind you of all that He is, all that He has, and all that He wants to share with you, His precious bride.

2. *"Your Kingdom come, your will be done." SURRENDER TO HIM!* Our King reigns — He always has and He always will. Today, the goodness of His kingdom is demonstrated wherever His will is known and followed. Pray that the King

will reign in your heart and do His will through your life this day (Mark 14:36, John 4:34, 5:30; Rom. 12:1-2, 1 Thess. 5:16-18).

3. *"Give us this day our daily bread."* RE-CEIVE HIS FULLNESS! Jesus, himself the Bread of life, longs to equip you with the riches and resources of His life. When you give yourself to Him, He gives himself to you. You become one with Him — not in the New Age sense where the human personality is absorbed into a pantheistic force — but in the privilege of sharing in His life. All that He is and has becomes available to you so that He can fulfill His purpose in you. This is covenant relationship, and it's far more wonderful than human thoughts can conceive (Matt. 6:33; John 6:35-63; Ps. 62:5-6; Eph. 3:14-19).

4. *"Forgive us as we forgive."* RECEIVE HIS CLEANSING! God calls us to "be holy" as He is holy. Ask Him to search your heart. Confess any sin He shows you. Thank Him for His forgiveness and receive His cleansing holy life. Praise Him for what He accomplished for you at the cross. There must be no hindrance to the biblical oneness between Him and you, nor between you and His other friends (Matt. 6:14-15; Heb. 4:14-16; James 5:16; 1 Pet. 1:16; 1 John 1:9, 3:2-3).

5. *"Deliver us from the evil one."* BATTLE IN PRAYER! Take hold of the spiritual victories Christ won for you at the cross. They become living realities when you count on them. So speak His Word in His authority and stand firm His mighty power against the enemies of the Kingdom (Exod. 14:13; 2 Chron. 20:6-15; Ps. 18; Matt. 16:19; Eph. 6:18; 1 John 4:4; Rev. 12:10-11).

6. *"For Yours is the Kingdom and the power and the glory forever!"* AFFIRM YOUR TRUST IN HIM! The Kingdom belongs to God, but He shares its riches now and forever with His children, friends and bride (all who are part of the true Church) who trust and follow. Unbounded blessings follow those who love Him enough to hear His heart, share His concerns, and walk in His purpose (Mark 11:22-24; John 15:7, 14:12-14; Phil. 4:4-7, 19; James 1:5-6, 4:3).

If, with all your heart, you pray through this outline and surrender your life into His loving hands, He will surely answer you — for you have asked according to His will (1 John 5:14-15). You are safe in Him, whether you live or die, for He surrounds you as an armor[28] and fills you with His very own life. Then you can stand with confidence on the wonderful promise He gives you in Romans 8:

What then shall we say to these things? If God *is* for us, who *can be* against us? He who did not spare His own Son, but delivered Him up for us all, how shall He not with Him also freely give us all things? . . . Who shall separate us from the love of Christ? *Shall* tribulation, or distress, or persecution, or famine, or nakedness, or peril, or sword? . . . Yet in all these things we are more than conquerors through Him who loved us. For I am persuaded that neither death nor life, nor angels nor principalities nor powers, nor things present nor things to come, nor height nor depth, nor any other created thing, shall be able to separate us from the love of God which is in Christ Jesus our Lord (Rom. 8:31-39).

Endnotes

[1] Nancy Smith and Donna Maxfield, "Spiritual Quest in Beijing," *Good News,* November/December 1995, p. 34.

[2] James Redfield, *Celestine Prophecy* (New York, NY: Time Warner Company, 1993).

[3] Barbara Marx Hubbard, *Revelation* (Greenbrae, CA: The Foundation for Conscious Evolution), p. 111-112.

[4] Spoken at the Renaissance of Christian Spirituality at Grace Cathedral, San Francisco, March 24, 1995.

[5] Hubbard, p. 112.

[6] Hubbard, p. 234-5.

[7] See 1 Corinthians 14 and 2 Timothy 1:7.

[8] Arianna Huffington, *The Fourth Instinct* (New York, NY: Simon & Schuster, 1994), p. 21.

[9] Ibid., p. 27-28.

[10] Ibid., p. 47.

[11] Ibid., p. 29.

[12] Ibid., p. 20.

[13] Hubbard, p. 124.

[14] Some of those angelic helpers could have been God's true ministering angels. But, when people are oblivious to God's warnings and as ready for *any* spiritual experience as this circle of seekers was, their chances of meeting the counterfeit grows. Some experiences sounded ominously occult.

[15] Redfield, p. 240-242.

[16] Redfield, "Author's Note" opposite page 1.

[17] Aldous Huxley, *Brave New World* (New York, NY: HarperPerennial, 1932), p. 52.

[18] Robert Muller, *A Planet of Hope,* quoted in Robert Muller's *World Core Curriculum Journal*, Vol. 1 (Arlington, TX; The Robert Muller School, 1989), p. 1.

[19] "Women of the Spirit," *The Global Link Newsletter,* Vol. 20, 1995, p. 8.

[20] Thomas Sowell, "A Road to Hell Paved with Good Intentions," *Forbes,* January 17, 1994, p. 62.

[21] Hubbard, p. 294.

[22] God's protection: Numbers 14:9; Micah 1:11; Isaiah 22:8-9; Deuteronomy 8:6-20, 31:17; Ezra 8:22.

[23] The word "antichrist" is not actually used in the book of Revelation. It is used four times in John's first two letters.

[24] Matthew 5:10; 2 Timothy 2:12; Revelation 3:10.

[25] Matthew 6:5-6; 1 Corinthians 3; Revelation 14:1-5.

[26] Joni Eareckson Tada, *Heaven* (Grand Rapids, MI: Zondervan Publishing House, 1995), p. 99.

[27]Jane Hussey Larson, "Spiritual Ultrasound," *Lutheran Commentator,* November/December 1995, p. 6.

[28]Did you notice the similarities between the Lord's prayer and the outline of the armor of God in Ephesians 6:10-18? (chapter 3). Both begin by affirming the truth about God. Both include confession and cleansing, affirming His sufficiency, and the hope of eternity. Both will bring you into His presence, fill you with His life, and cover you with His protection — not because these words are a magic formula, but because our Father has promised to respond to His children who seek Him, His way.

Berit Kjos

An insightful author and popular conference speaker, Berit Kjos (pronounced Chos) began examining the differences between New Age thought and the Bible in the 1970s. Her research led her and her husband to develop study materials for church groups, and alert parents to the introduction of earth-based spirituality in public schools.

The mother of three sons, Berit prefers to investigate thoroughly the books she writes, thus bringing a fresh and relevant presentation to her audiences. A native of Norway, she lives in California.

Index

a

B

C

D

R

S

T

y